the Spiritual Vixen's Guide
to an Unapologetic Life

the
Spiritual
Vixen's

Guide to an
Unapologetic Life

Maureen Muldoon

SHE WRITES PRESS

Published 2018
Printed in the United States of America
ISBN: 978-1-63152-447-9
ISBN: 978-1-63152-448-6
Library of Congress Control Number: 2018948228

For information, address:
She Writes Press
1569 Solano Ave #546
Berkeley, CA 94707

She Writes Press is a division of SparkPoint Studio, LLC.

Cover and interior design by Tabitha Lahr

To Will for asking twice.

Epigraph

What we hunger for perhaps more than anything else is to be known in our full humanness, and yet that is often just what we also fear more than anything else.

—Frederick Buechner, *Telling Secrets*

Contents

Foreword

Dear Divine,

I tuck my chin, bow my head, and surrender all that I am to all You will have me be. I bow my head, my heart, my desires, and my agendas to Your will. I trust that You know me and love me as I continue to make my way home to peace. I trust that Your agents of love go with me. I trust that I will see miracles where I once saw lack and limitations, and that I will be assisted in solutions where I once saw dead ends. I commit to remembering that I am immersed in Your holy ecstasy and audaciousness where all things are possible, plentiful, and perfect.

I thank you for this day of miraculous encounters. May I always remember that this Grace is offered to me not just for my own good, but so that I may be a fearless extension of Your Love.

Amen!

—Maureen Muldoon

Preface

My first memory fades in like morning sun through a sheer curtain, and I can't see the importance at first. I am three or four, standing on tippy toes on a church kneeler. My little hands holding tight to the pew in front of me I strain to peek and capture a glance. My senses are flooded with stained glass and women's perfume.

I pull my nose over the pew; it holds a mystical, old scent, of wood, wax polish and incense of crushed cloves and rosary beads. I open my mouth to taste it then draw back disappointed, scraping my tongue of the pungent taste. My tired arms release my grip as I slip down to sit on the kneeler. I wipe my mouth of the wretched taste that holds the odd combination of the bitterness of soap and the earthiness of fingernail dirt.

Still, I love church. It's a place of color and beauty. The men all smile and the ladies wear lipstick and everyone sings together and wears hats. You have to be quiet and sit still in church, but I don't mind. There is so much to take in that I am struck still anyway.

I am five when I begin to feel like something is missing. Something is tremendously off balance. My sisters sit silently as the priest drones on and I wonder where their voices have gone.

At home they hum and bubble and prattle. They spill over with sounds and songs, sentences and sermons. But here in the church they are silenced. I see my younger brothers up on the altar, carrying the gifts and ringing the bell, I see the old men passing baskets for the collection. I search the pews and the rafters. I find not even an echo of the feminine Divine.

In second grade, I learn the prayers *Glory be to the Father and to the Son.* Where are the mother and the daughter? Where are the priests that look like me, and why have they been exiled?

Although I knew that my sisters' voices could never truly be silenced. I witnessed them systematically turned down and buried. As a child, I was helpless. As a woman, I am responsible and that is why I have written this book.

I can no longer tolerate the second-hand roles and the bitter injustice pressed upon us under what should have been a holy sanctuary. I stand in my commitment to unearth the voice of female spiritual authority. I will ruffle the feathers and shake the roots 'till a healing is heard and heralded. For until the desecration of the Divine feminine is put to rest, the world will go on warring and weeping.

Today I am called not just to wipe the bad taste from my lips, but to spit truth. To free my mother tongue and speak of, as, and for the feminine Divine.

Until we heal the illusion of a widowed father God, we will not have peace. It is time to lift the veil and break the gag order, banish the self-doubt and reclaim our spiritual authority. We can't start with men. We need to empower women from inside the sacred tribe, through recognition and celebration.

Our bodies, which have been used to condemn, are innocent. Now is the time to strip down to our most holy self and come naked and empowered to the temples. Freed of all the blame and shame that is not ours to carry, and was never authored by God.

Being back in New York was reminding me of who we had been, and how far we now were from those star-crossed lovers.

We had come back only for a holiday visit. Two years earlier, we had moved from New York to Los Angeles to try our luck in La La Land as actors. I was not all that excited by the move. I was a Jersey girl with a huge crush on New York, and I had managed to book acting work in the leaner market. But Reed was adamant. He had heard about the abundance of shows and productions and was convinced that we needed to move to Hollywood.

Back In New York, the air felt lighter, the horizons familiar, and the sounds comforting. It was hard to think about returning to LA, to our small apartment and crumbling marriage. I wanted to hold onto this snow globe scene with Owen. I held my breath in hopes that it would last forever. I lifted my face to the skies and sent out a silent plea as a soft river of tears trickled into my ears. I could not stay frozen. I would have to move. I was fumbling in the dark, feeling for a non-existent light switch. I felt unanchored, unprepared, and slightly unwilling to admit that my marriage was ending.

I fought to bring myself back to the moment, the sweet whispers of my son's reverence for snow, and I tried not to think of the innocent casualties. I wish I could say that I prayed, but the truth is that God was a concept as far away as the stars. I had left that fairytale years before back in New Jersey. Prodded into cynicism with Bruce Springsteen's warnings: *Praying in vain for a savior to rise from these streets.* I spent my high school days bobbing my head to the lyrics as I sat in the bucket seat of my boyfriend's Camaro, hiking up my Catholic school skirt, and defiantly singing along to forbidden lyrics.

I blame Sea-Monkeys for the chip on my shoulder. There was a time before Sea-Monkeys that I had believed in a savior, sent out prayers and orchestrated holy processions to intervene for my mother and her battle with cancer. Around the same time, I had saved my money for Sea-Monkeys. The advertisement showed a cool underwater family with pot-bellies and little crowns on their heads. They were magnificent, magical, and I wanted them to be mine. But when they arrived they looked more like floating fish parts. It was a terrible moment. I remember lying in bed and realizing that I had been duped. In that moment, I had a revelation that God was most likely a shiny fable too. No wonder my prayers were not working.

So, I became a card carrying prodigal daughter with a self-will the size of Kansas. Who needed a broken-down God? I would fix this or figure it out on my own. God was the emperor's new clothes, the wizard of Oz, the world's greatest scam artist. I was done with praying. I had tossed my last tearful pleas to the heavens. God was the phony king of the Sea-Monkeys, and that's all there was to it.

The next morning we left the beauty of the snow and flew back to LA. Reed had flown home earlier for work and would be picking us up at the airport. It was a long flight. Owen was tired. When we arrived, my cell phone let me know that Reed was on his way. An hour passed and then another. When he finally arrived, it was with an exaggerated hug for Owen and an icy shoulder for me. I tried to find his eyes, search for clues, to figure out what I had done or forgotten to do, what I had missed. The more I searched, the less I found. It was a painful experiment in seeing how many times I was willing to touch the hot oven. Turns out, many.

Reed rushed us to his illegal parking space, tossed the bags into the car, and we took a silent drive back to our apartment. With my stomach aching and my eyes stinging, I felt confused, frightened, and ready to fold. My breath was shallow, my mind vacant and I sat, a shadow of myself, trying to hold on with all I had.

We pulled in, and Reed carried Owen upstairs to our apartment. I lingered in the parking garage. It was cold, damp, and quiet.

I couldn't help feeling like I was being buried alive. I took my time bringing in the luggage from the car. It was a way to avoid being in the apartment with Reed. I tried making conversation, to break the ice and warm up the room, but his replies were staccato and stoic and seemed to suck the air from everything. I was suffocating and yet at the same time struggling to stay. Like treading water with a foot on my head.

None of it made any sense. This mean and distant behavior was not my husband. This was not the man who had once gazed at me like I was made of stardust. This was not the guy who built me flower boxes and took me on a helicopter ride over New York for my twenty-fourth birthday. This was not the starry-eyed lover who had sworn his devotion and whispered with conviction that nothing would ever change that.

But something had changed. Something had been said or done to flip all that on its head. The rug had been pulled and the silence of the canary was deafening. Our apartment felt like everything had already been rolled up and tagged to sell. It was getting harder and harder to breathe.

I needed air and was grateful to have the excuse to leave and get the bags. I made a few trips with baby bags, umbrella stroller, and gifts we had received from the holiday visit. Before taking in the last bags, I decided to just sit in the car for a while. I needed a little solitude to figure things out. I had never sat in the driver's seat or driven his—*our* car because I couldn't drive stick. This should have been a big clue for me as to why my life was so off track. I was figuratively, emotionally, and literally not in the driver's seat.

But for some reason, when I went to sit in the car this time, I opened the driver's side and crawled into the bucket seat. Leaning my head back to rest for a moment, I felt small and strange. The pain I felt was debilitating enough to pull from me, not so much a prayer, but a plea. A sincere surrender. "If there is someone, anyone, some God, some force or source, some angel, saint or sage, I'll take it. I'll take anything. Please help me figure out this riddle." I closed my eyes, took a deep breath, and suddenly I heard a voice. It was not outside myself, but kind of in my head.

"Look in the side compartment of the car door." It was faint but clear, and it made me open my eyes and sit up. I looked around to try and make sense of it. The parking garage was quiet, not a soul in sight, so I tried to shake off the odd instructions and settle back down to rest. I was not a snooper. I had no secrets, nothing to hide, and no reason to suspect Reed of hiding anything.

But as I sat there staring at the windshield, I heard it again.

"Look in the side compartment of the car door." At first, I thought what does that even mean? What's the side compartment of the car door? Cars have lots of doors. The glove compartment? The middle console? My hand moved instinctively to the armrest on the driver's door and flipped up the fake top. I heard myself gasp in surprise. I was honestly unaware that there was a side compartment in the driver's door.

I took a moment then reached inside. My hand connected with some paper or note and something else. I pulled out a letter and a set of keys with a silver charm in the shape of a heart. The notepaper held a sweet fragrance and the handwriting was distinctly feminine. It began as a thank you note. The mysterious author was thanking Reed for watching her home while she was in Thailand. Her letter included the necessary codes to get into her home, the numbers to reach her in Thailand, and "all of her love." It was the final offering that set off my inner alarms.

My thinking began to warp as I tried to make sense of it. I watched my mind protect itself with irrational rationalizations. This note was not his. It's something he'd been holding for a friend so that his friend's wife wouldn't find it.

Or maybe this lady, who is off visiting Thailand, maybe she is really just a friend, maybe a friendly friend who is very generous with her love, or maybe, maybe, maybe . . . the more I scrambled to turn this tragedy into tolerable truth, the more I began slipping, sliding, and falling down. Though I thought I had hit bottom, I was suddenly free falling like Alice down the rabbit hole, tumbling down with nothing to hold onto and no bottom in sight. Blindsided and sideswiped, my thoughts plummeted into an abyss. And yet somehow, I watched myself, or at least my body, get up. I don't remember tears, just slow methodical movement. I am sure I was in shock.

I walked, wounded, from the garage in a zombie-like autopilot. Thoughts running through me like water through a sieve.

With the note in hand, I made my way down my block, keenly aware of the effort it took to keep moving. I had no real conscious idea of where I was going. The odd little voice pulled me on with gentle instructions, and so I followed. I walked to the corner and into the copier place and watched myself make twenty copies of the letter then stuff them into a rented mailbox, along with the key and heart-shaped charm.

This was not my plan, this was some divinely orchestrated thought process. If things were done in my style, I would have run raging to the apartment, flung open the door, and confronted him with this evidence. I would have cried and screamed and accused. It would have been loud and ugly. Not like this. Although it felt jagged, there was also some precision to it all. And oddly some relief, some answers to all the riddles, some reason for all the frigidness. It began making sense. My husband was having an affair.

Back in the apartment, I handed him the original letter and watched him rip it into a million little scraps and then set them on fire in the kitchen sink, the ashes floating in slow motion and falling to rest on the Formica countertops. I stayed calm.

He asked me for the key, and I bargained for the truth. "The key is safely stashed away with twenty other copies of the letter," I told him. And for some reason it was this news that caused him to confess.

"We're just friends, and she's just Miss Universe. Well, she was Miss Thailand first, then she became Miss Universe. And her breasts are so perfect, they have to be fake."

The final line of his eloquent speech reverberated back at me in a thousand voices.

"Her breasts are so perfect, they have to be fake."

Like a plummeting elevator, my world soared down and then came to a sudden stop and tilted sideways. What? What was he saying? What was I hearing? Who brags to his wife about the beauty of his lover's breasts? I briefly tried to imagine and then did my best *not* to imagine the beauty of the breasts that turn a man into a total dipshit, so drunk on lust that he would gloat to his wife about his sexual conquest.

"Miss Universe," he whispered as if he had won the prized pig at a state fair. Crossing his arms over his chest he tucked his hands into his armpits, rocked back on his heels, and shook his head at the floor. Then with a slight blush and a sacred tone he repeated once more, "Can you believe it? Miss Universe."

I placed my hand over my mouth to hold back my confusion and shock. I had never before watched anyone go mad. Was this really my life? Was I seriously being dumped for Miss Universe? Miss flippin' Universe? How did this even happen? How many Miss Universes were there? There can't be that many and how many are even datable, still alive, not married, and not currently undergoing some form of plastic surgery? As my mind fluttered in the unlikely mathematics of it all, he kept talking. But I stopped listening. I began a new calculation of how I was going to move on from this moment with the least amount of scar tissue.

And then things got weirder. First, due to wild winds and rain, not normal weather in sunny LA, all the electricity in our building went out. In my youth, blackouts were filled with searches for candles and batteries and the phone number for the pizza guy. But on this day, we were barely fazed. Yes, of course the electricity would go out.

Then in the middle of this very dark hour, my former boyfriend from New Jersey, Phil, called. I picked up. After a brief, "Hey, how ya doin'?" he asked if we could help him out. He was on his way back home from a trip to Thailand and got stuck at LAX. Newark airport had lost all power due to some work that was being done, so all flights to Newark were canceled. He needed a place to stay the night.

"What? Wait. Seriously?" I looked around the room for a hidden camera. Was this some odd new reality show? A horrible joke? A nightmare? "You're coming from Thailand? Are you kidding me?" I asked with pointed accusation as if he were somehow in on this warped script. Phil's voice came back, tired but totally sincere.

"No, I'm not kidding. I don't know anyone else in LA, and I kinda need you to help me out." Honestly, it was good to hear his voice. He was from my native Jersey tribe and could provide me with a dose of clarity in the midst of this chaos.

It baffled me even more that the universe sent me this old sweetheart on such a heartless day. Phil and I had found each other after his dad died of a heart attack and my mother had passed from breast cancer. We were both teenagers at the time, and our similar life lessons catapulted us into a premature adulthood that most kids our age didn't understand. Of course, I would help him out. We had walked each other through a nightmare, and bonds like that can never be broken.

I sent Reed to pick Phil up at the airport and sat down on our sad futon couch, attempting to will all the puzzle pieces back together. All the nights Reed had come home late, the fighting, the constant cold shoulder, and unkindness all seemed so obvious now. Of course, he was having an affair. I was shocked at how shocked I was.

When they arrived at our apartment, Phil entered first, coming through the doorway with a huge Buddha statue strapped to his back. It was carved from beautiful dark wood that looked like walnut.

He had checked all his bags except the Buddha statue. He sat down on our couch beaming at his Buddha as he rambled on in a kind and comical way about the remarkable beauty of the girls from Thailand. My husband shot me a knowing look as if to say, "See? It's hard to deny." I waited patiently for an alarm to go off, some warped buzzer to wake me up. This could not be my life.

The synchronicities of the day, and now this large wooden Buddha placed auspiciously in the middle of my living room, brought me no comfort. The wooden expression contently stared back at me with the smile of Mona Lisa. What did it mean? It unnerved and intrigued me . . . like a sticky, spiritual Rubik's Cube. What was the Universe trying to tell me? I knew there was a message mingled with this madness, but my mind was too twisted to figure it out.

Reed suggested that Phil and I go grab some dinner while he watched Owen. Phil was confused to have my husband pushing us out the door together.

"I am not sure I would be so cool with my wife having dinner with an ex-boyfriend," he confessed over a glass of wine. I nodded because it sounded so normal and refreshing. Before I could stop myself, a wave of warm thick tears rolled forward. "Oh shit, Maureen. What happened?" I shared the series of events that took us to that moment, but it felt like I had only a few pieces of a huge jigsaw puzzle and was being asked to explain what it should look like. The truth was, I had no idea what had happened or how we had gotten to this place.

"Are you kidding me? Miss Thailand, and now I am coming back from Thailand? This is crazy. What does it mean?" he asked.

I stared at him in silence.

And then with a little more compassion he asked, "So what are you going to do? Will you be moving back to New Jersey?"

I had no answer for that one either. We both studied the air between us, lost in the question. And then, because I knew that he would completely understand, I confessed.

"I'm devastated." He nodded, and I saw a flash of that brave boy who had found his father on his beauty salon floor dead from a heart attack.

"You may be devastated," he finally replied, "but you are also devastatingly strong, and you have a kid and you are going to get through this. If anyone can, Maureen, you can. You know how to land on your feet."

I nodded not because I believed him, but because I wanted to believe him. His words of encouragement were just what I needed to hear. No matter if they were true of not, I was so glad that the Universe had stranded him in LA for the night.

After dinner, Phil and I went back to my apartment, met up with Reed, and closed out the day with a short and awkward conversation, all pretending everything was fine. Then we went to sleep exhausted by the roller coaster of emotions, the comings and goings of Thailand, the finding and burning of letters, the discovery of the silver heart and the unplanned visit from Buddha. We each slid off to our own hibernations—Phil and his Buddha statue on the futon in the living room, Owen in his bed, and Reed and me in ours. None of us really wanted to be there, but we had no place else to go. In the morning, we got up. That was it. We had made it through that first night, and there was no going back. Which only left forward. From this morning moment, we were all on our own, and it was every man and woman for themselves.

Phil lifted his Buddha statue and left for the airport. Reed gathered his workout equipment into a stranded shopping cart and moved in with a neighbor. I packed up Owen and all our belongings and began to make my way to a new life. I found a back-house bungalow in Santa Monica where I would test the waters of being a single mom, take up an affair with yoga, work as an actress, and drive a new-to-me 1964 Ford Falcon convertible around town with its sparkly blue, Earl Scheib paint job. I entered what was, and remains, one of the most magical chapters of my life.

It turns out, magical chapters can start with really sucky endings that aren't actually endings at all.

I am not sure what I had been expecting to find during this particular portion of my journey, but I know I was not expecting to find my own strength. The excavation was slow, but constant. Every day I met with a million reasons to duck and cover; and every day, I got up if only for lack of a better option and stepped into a life that I had no map for. I had never lived alone. I had never had someone else's life completely and solely dependent on mine. I had never imagined myself to be that capable. Reed's parting words rang in my ears:

"You are in for a shock. You're not going to be able to make it on your own out there. No one's going to want you. Who wants damaged goods?" I was so turned around that I had no way of knowing if he said these things to harm me or warn me. All I knew was that I needed to prove them wrong.

I could accept that I had been tossed into the deep end of the ocean, but I was not willing to accept that I would drown. I would tread water for the rest of my fucking life if I had to, but this shipwreck was not going to take me under. This was not just for myself, this was for Owen. I could not, would not, fail.

I surprised myself in a thousand ways that first year. The girl who had been married was so different from the girl who was abandoned. I liked the new version better. Her gumption was boundless, her flare authentic, her resourcefulness admirable.

I had become a girl on fire and was on course to rise as a Spiritual Vixen. It wasn't overnight. It was a consistent slog as I approached day after day learning to put one foot in front of the other, walking my way back out of hell and beginning to trust that still, small voice within me. Along the way, I was getting to know a version of myself, the one I had lost touch with over the years. The kid who believed in miracles and Sea-Monkeys and God.

I let myself be opened, and opened again, and again, and again. Like a never-ending nesting doll. Drilling down deeper to myself, my core, my truth. Questioning everything, leaving nothing unexamined. Shedding and surrendering over and over with each new wave of pain and paradox.

In that willingness, something happened. Something holy bloomed from the wasteland. I developed an appreciation for things falling down. Snowflakes will fall, and teardrops will fall, and eventually even the most beautiful breasts will fall. Marriages, like buildings, will topple and fall, just like torn scraps of love letters tumble and fall. And ashes, yes ashes, the ashes will fall, and we, we will all fall down.

I came to learn that "down" was simply a resting place, not a destination. This ground zero of my life was not a bottom, it was a beginning. On shaky knees and weary haunches, I would enter a year filled with gifts, guidance, and golden wisdom. A year of dismantling demons and ravishing resurrections and it all started with this strange connection to this inner teacher.

This is my story, a sharing of the wisdom I learned on the way back up. The spiritual insights that I gleaned in my darkest hour. I offer them to you with complete faith that they will work to awaken you to a more empowered state. But please know that an authentic artisan life does not come by way of recipes and formulas. You need to trust your own poetry and become a "bin diver."

What's a bin diver? When I was a kid, my sisters and I would head off like pirates to the local secondhand shop in our town. For me, this place held big magic. It was like no other place I had ever been. There were serious hidden treasures to be found—beaded belts, strands of pearls, hats, boots, buttons, and ball gowns—all with such great potential and possibility. All of them screaming to have a second life. I fell in love a hundred times before even getting to the dressing room. I noticed that my approach to the thrift shop made my sisters blush and giggle. They started to affectionately refer to me as "a bin diver."

My elegant sisters would look over the shelves and racks with dignity, while I would dive to the bottom of every bin and bucket with the zeal of a dog on the scent of chicken livers. There were gems to be found, and I wanted to discover them. I did not play it safe. I wore my hunger on my sleeve. I was not always sure what I was looking for, but I was sure that I would find it. And I did. I always came up with something magnificent.

Now you can't really make someone a bin diver. But you can encourage even the safest of creatives to try on a bit of reckless abandon to inspire them to get to the bottom of their being and bring up the good stuff. I am asking you to let the invitations and suggestions at the end of each chapter take you deep into your own stories. May you bring up some valuable pearls of your own.

No matter where you are in your journey, we can all benefit from honoring our journeys in the hopes of reclaiming our most unapologetic lives. The caterpillar grows up to be a beautiful butterfly. Sand is the seed of pearls. Coal is only the first stage of brilliant diamonds. And you, my dear, are the raw ingredient of a powerful Spiritual Vixen. May you rise.

⁓ TOOL ⁓

Dear Divine
There is an internal intelligence that knows your optimal
potential. Whether you call it God, Goddess, or Guru does
not matter. What matters is that you connect with it. There
is only one way to reap the benefits of this wisdom: Be still
and know. Stillness is not just for the body. Stillness is a
surrendering of all the thinking. This tool will help clear the
space for grace.

⁓ DO THIS ⁓

Every morning, take out a pen and journal. Take a breath and surrender your will to God's will. Then write, "Dear Divine, What would you have me do today?" Listen for the Voice and just take dictation. Try to stay away from a "to do" list or pushing through your own agenda. Your higher power's direction is not going to sound like what you would expect. Its direction is simple and clear, and it never asks you to do anything that you are not fully capable of. If you are not comfortable writing "Dear Divine," then go ahead and write whatever name you give to your internal Guidance. It does not matter what you call it, just *that* you call it, early and often.

This practice is first for a reason. On this practice, all the other tools and inspirations will rest. Seek first God, and all else is given. The key word is "first." It's time to get your spiritual priorities in order.

This is no small thing. You're an important and integral piece of the great mosaic of God, and without you God is incomplete.

Devoting yourself to this spiritual practice is the cornerstone of creating a life that is good, beautiful, and holy. It is from this daily holy communion that you will receive your most authentic blessings, generous inspirations, and immaculate conceptions—concepts that have not been tainted by the weary regulations and regurgitations of the world. This is fresh baked bread that was created just for you. Get on it!

The practice is simple. You can't mess it up, unless you don't do it. It will take less than five minutes a day, and it is the first thing that you get to do. No exceptions. No excuses. Put some skin in the game, be a bin diver. Don't just go to God when your ass is on fire. Make this a daily spiritual vitamin, a habit like brushing your teeth.

And when you fall away, as you will, just notice and begin again. You will find many reasons not to practice. Many opportunities to busy yourselves with alternative altars and unholy distractions. Do your best to stay consistent with this sacred conversation.

So there you have it, the first and most important tool is connection. As you go within, you will never go without. You have a benevolent internal compass who knows everything about you, is madly in love with you, and is ready to reveal all the shortcuts to your most purposeful outcome, why wouldn't you check in with Her first?

Chapter 2

Signs and Symbols

In quietness are all things answered.
—*A Course in Miracles*

The New Year was ringing in all around me, and there I was freshly dumped for Miss Universe, doing my best not to absorb the sad script casting me in the role of loser. In the sea of New Year's celebrations, resolutions, and songs of new beginnings, it was hard to find a silver lining in my reality. I felt painfully pixelated, shrouded in darkness and frozen in time. Plus my creative and morbid mind had a way of driving me into the abyss. My marriage had failed; I was getting divorced. I would never make anything of myself and would surely spend the rest of my life scraping by on borrowed bread crumbs. This was not just a voice in my head, or the perverse proclamation from my "wasband," this was the subtle expression that seemed to sit sideways on the faces of my sisters, poking its head from the pews at church, branding me with its sorrowful gaze. "Oh, poor Maureen, what is she going to do?" I did my best to fan my inner flame in hopes of holding back all of the communal doubts. I felt heavy with the weight of grief and further burdened with the pity piled on me by every well-meaning encounter.

Plus, and this is embarrassing to admit, I had a new-found obsession with breasts. It no doubt sprung from my husband's reverence for Miss Universe's "perfect assets." My own breasts had shrunken severely after breast feeding, and I had a tiny mad idea that if I still had breasts, I would still be married. I felt flat in every way.

This sticky thought reached out to me from every bill-board and peeked at me from the cover of every magazine in the grocery line. Cleavage! I was swimming in a sea of perfect breasts. No matter where I looked they were there mocking me. LA is known for its bevy of *Baywatch* busts and Marilyn mounds. There was no getting away from it, I lived in the mecca of mammary glands.

To compensate, I began wearing what felt like full-on bullet-proof, padded bras that turned me into a sweaty, self-conscious, sweater girl. It started small, a simple soft padded underwire, and before I knew it I was wearing two at a time with the helpful addition of silicone chicken cutlets that I sent away for in the mail. These flesh colored fun bags promised cleavage and confidence; I was possessed. I gained great compassion for the toupee-touting, comb-over crew. This self inflicted facade made it easy to side-step any romantic invitations that came my way. Having someone find out the truth behind the twin peaks was not something I was willing to deal with. So . . . there was that.

My finances were equally unimpressive. Doubts wrestled me from my sleep and left me calculating numbers on my bedroom ceiling. The morose monsters from under the bed moaned mad musings that left me frozen. What was I going to do now that I was getting divorced? In my Catholic community, this particular marital status that I found myself checking on rental agreement forms and job applications held the same designation as being a leper, a marked woman, an outcast. To add weight to the worry, I was also a mother with eight hundred bucks in my pocket, no savings, no credit history, no real child support. Reed was not Owen's legal father. And, though he had played the role brilliantly for the past four years, he was the first to bring it up when I suggested that he help out with child support. He coughed up a hundred dollars a week, which would just cover Owen's pre-school tuition.

And as for my employability, I had graduated from high school and enrolled at the American Academy of Dramatic Arts. They did not teach real life skills at the Academy. So basically, I had my master's in "mime" and "playtime." Little did I know how handy that would come in.

My single, childless actor friend Skye, who lived on ecstasy and adventure, observed me with morbid curiosity as she chain smoked her Camels and gulped down mugs of coffee at our kitchen table. She had come to visit me with her friend Bean.

For a while, Skye had rented out our backroom. Now due to our impending move she was here to pick up the stuff that we had been storing for her. Her friend Bean was a model who was skinny as a string bean. I am not sure if that is how she got her nickname, but that was how I remembered it.

Bean always seemed to be fighting a laughing fit, like she was perpetually baked. Having her pop by with Skye during this jagged moment was a little annoying. She did not have a drop of malice in her bones, but her youthful effervescence made me feel twice as old and ten times as heavy. She was the one to introduce Skye and me to the theatre group. This might have been why Reed didn't like Bean or Skye. He hated the theatre group and was intensely jealous.

"I bet there's a bunch of great-looking guys there. I bet that's the real reason you go to the group," Reed would suggest.

It's funny to think that the whole time he was pointing the finger at me, he was screwing around.

I loved the group and never missed a Monday. I was so grateful for the community and connection that it offered me— especially when I had felt so disconnected. These were the days when Owen and I would go to the parks in Beverly Hills and play in the sand box. I had hoped to meet other mothers but only found Mexican nannies. Although they seemed great, I didn't speak Spanish, and they had no time to teach me.

I'd sit on the cement curb that lined the sand pit as the LA sun fried eggs on my head and listened to their laughter, smiling kindly in their direction, pretending like I could understand them. They would slap each other's thighs and share bags of green grapes and tamales wrapped in wax paper. Everything about their tight tribe only made me miss my roots all the more and crave for community.

Having Skye live with us was helpful, but it turned out that she honestly just needed a place to store her stuff. She spent nights at her boyfriend's house, and days running around from gigs to auditions to meeting to classes. She thrived on caffein-ated chaos and always seemed to have a million creative balls in the air. Skye was eternally busting with ideas, inspirations, and conversation; they seemed to flow from her like a river.

We had became fast friends five years earlier when we were both shipped from New York to LA by our acting manager, Barbara Jarret. We ended up as roommates for two months during pilot season.

Pilot season is the time of year when all the studios pro-duced a bunch of new shows. Each show begins with a pilot episode. If the pilot episode is good, it gets picked up and is given a season run.

At sixteen, Skye was an old pro at this. She had already booked a couple pilots and even had one of her shows picked up.

It was really no surprise—she was stunning and sure of

herself, a lovely and lethal combination. We would be room-mates for our time in LA She was a New Yorker, sixteen years old, and I was twenty-two and from New Jersey. But it felt like she was older than me. She bested me in style, street smarts, and cigarette smoke. Hers were Camels; mine were Merits. I was six years older than she and yet felt like the kid sister.

She spoke Kerouac, Kandinsky, and Rilke. I barely spoke Springsteen. She'd drop poetry into our conversations in the way most people left pauses.

Have known the evenings, mornings, afternoons,
I have measured out my life with coffee spoons.

I'd smile and nod and wonder what the fuck she was talking about. She'd press pages passionately to my palms. Poems and prose and passages of songs. She spoke using all her limbs, her black mop of hair dancing around her head, her bright blue eyes like two wells holding fire and conviction and entitlement.

She walked like she was raised on the red carpet, which she was. She had starred in her own TV show by the time she was fourteen. Her confidence was devastating. Unlike the aloof, lean-limbed girls we would meet in the audition rooms, Skye's bravado did not live on the surface, it went straight to the bone marrow of who she was.

She personified limitlessness, and her name was perfect. During our time as roommates, she would impress upon me the importance of an extensive vocabulary. She chased words like a junkie and was the most voracious reader I'd ever met. It seemed to me that she knew everyone and everything there was to know. I was completely taken by her.

The bond that grew between us was as instantaneous as it was unlikely. It was more twisted than sisters, less casual than cousins, more intimate than friends. I popped the pimples on her back, lent her cash I didn't have, and helped her construct elaborate lies to untangle her from the sordid relationships she sometimes found herself entwined in. I am not sure who else I would do those things for. But I did them for her.

She was a rambler, a gambler, a comedian, and con artist. When you meet someone like that, you have an obligation to pledge your allegiance and ensure their safety like a national treasure. And you're never quite sure what you're protecting them from, at least that's how I felt with Skye. I just had an intuition that I had to stick close 'cause she might not last. Everything was being burnt up and at both ends; it was hard to imagine how someone could maintain that type of charisma. But she did.

She sat across from me and spoke silent monologues with her eyes. The truth was, I was grateful to see her. She was one of the few people in LA that I had any real history with. It was helpful to be able to get an honest assessment on my situation.

Skye had an appreciation for cats who could land on their feet, but the current catapult was causing her sincere concern. Would I stick this landing?

"Miss Universe? Jesus! So what are you going to do?" I shrugged in silence.

Bean rested her chin on her hand, tucked her blonde hair behind her ear

"Are you going to stay here?" Bean asked with wide eyes and pinched brows. It was such a pretty face, and I felt guilty for having wrinkled it. "'Cause being a single mom, ain't easy," she added.

She had just been raised on too much TV and watched me like a daytime drama. I had hooked my wagons to Hollywood hopes. I was living in a land that lavished the young and free, an industry that celebrated the feisty and fierce. I was twenty-eight, and in my mind I was neither young, free, feisty, nor fierce. What I was, was fucked. And royally so.

"Of course she is staying here." Skye answered for me. "Maureen, you will figure it out, but you just have to figure it out."

"Thanks for clearing that up." I nodded and then, to erase the worry from their brows, "I'll be fine," I told them.

"Oh sure you will be," Bean assured me. "I was raised by a single mom you know. Which was hard as dick for her, but you know, great for me, I got away with so much shit." She smacked her forehead and laughed until she folded in on herself.

"Thanks, Bean" I said, forcing a smile and silently hating her for her honesty and happiness.

The notion that I was a hair away from homelessness kept a hot fire under my feet. That morbid thought was branded into me with every rattling shopping cart that made its way down the alley behind our apartment building. I was on a slippery slope, every day facing a billion reasons why it might be wiser to duck and cover than to rise and rally. I could always go home to New Jersey and get a job with my dad as a secretary. Or I could stay in LA and try to navigate life in the shifty sands of showbiz.

It'd been a while since I had made an independent decision, and now I was faced with an army of them. They marched around my mind and made it hard to breathe. Where would we live? Where would I work? Where would Owen go to school? And the hardest question of all, how would we even make it? I needed a sign.

As kids, my father had taught us to pick a sign or symbol to represent our mother after her death so that when we saw it, we would know that she was still around and all was well. The world was stripping me down to the bone, I needed to stay open and pay attention. I knew the Divine would converse with me in a million different ways if I stayed open to the conversation that would come in signs and symbols and synchronicities.

It was an interesting experiment to have no cash, no income, no home, no family within three-thousand miles, and no clue how to navigate this new territory. Not too surprisingly,

Reed was of no help at all. As obvious as this should have been, I was not prepared. You take things for granted inside a relationship, like, "of course you will be helping me pack up all our stuff." It's disconcerting to find that once the jig is up, all the normal acts of decency go with it, and you begin doing things to the other person that you would never do to your worst enemy.

"You need to find a new place and be out by the end of the month. Our lease is up, and I don't want any of our stuff." I listened to his voice on our answering message and felt my heart hit the floor. I played the message back a couple times to be sure I had heard him correctly. It was not just the sudden eviction notice. It was the cold way he had washed his hands of everything. I felt gutted by the realization that the past four years of our life could be so disposable.

But I had no time to sweat the small stuff; I needed to pack our three-bedroom apartment, get a job, find a place to live, enroll Owen in a preschool, and move all by the end of the month. Great.

I did my best to go on autopilot. But I wasn't kidding anyone. My emotions seeped out at unconventional moments. I would burst into tears while filling out rental agreements or paying the pizza delivery boy. It was not pretty. I wept myself to sleep, and then woke up early to gather empty cardboard boxes from the local supermarket and sort through our belongings until the next tearful tsunami washed in.

The good news was that Reed was a minimalist, and it didn't actually take me too long to get through all our belongings. It went pretty smoothly until I stumbled on the pictures and videos of our wedding day, and then I began to feel nauseous and dizzy. I placed all those albums, and the ones from our road trips and other romantic adventures, into a box and set it off to the side. I could not bring myself to accept that it was over.

In the midst of this shitstorm, I had stopped eating and weight was melting off me like May snow. I had no appetite, and when I did eat, it was hard to keep it down. It was like I was in a funhouse where the floor kept falling out, the walls kept shifting and the images in the mirrors were warped and upside down. My mind was scrambled and nothing made sense.

I felt like I was losing my faculties. Even in all the pain, I actually still loved my husband, or I thought I did. Plus, I couldn't fathom being divorced. No one in my family had been divorced; I would surely be tossed from the tribe. I needed to do whatever I could to try and save this sinking ship. I set up an appointment with a marriage counselor and begged Reed to come with me. He agreed, and we set a time to meet.

The office was in Beverly Hills, and the therapist was a no-nonsense woman in her sixties. I sat in her office and made small talk as we waited for Reed. After fifteen minutes, she looked over at the clock and suggested that we should get started.

I took a breath and began to share the story as it was revealed to me in the past week, the letter, the lies, the lacerations that I was feeling. She nodded knowingly. When I filled her in on the details of Miss Universe and her noteworthy breasts, she seemed to get a kick out of it, like I was explaining the plot to a weird romantic comedy.

Once I was finished she asked me a question: "So what do you want?"

I wasn't prepared and just looked back at her with wide eyes. "Do you want to stay in the marriage?" she continued. Without hesitation, I nodded my head yes. She sank back into her oversized chair, sized me up with a tight-lipped look, and then she gently suggested that to stay in the marriage I would need to accept the situation.

"Just accept that your husband has a girlfriend," she added in a very matter-of-fact way. I leaned in for clarity, doubling down on my confusion.

"Just accept that my husband has a girlfriend?" I repeated, trying to interpret her suggestion.

"Yes." She nodded again, adding, "This type of thing is actually a standard arrangement for most marriages that I work with." My stomach churned, and my blood boiled. I was not interested in the standard. That type of agreement would never sit well with my soul. I may not have known exactly what it was that I wanted, but I was pretty clear on what I didn't want. I didn't want to accept that my husband had a girlfriend.

Then, before closing her notebook, she offered me one more jewel of advice. Find out what he really cares about and care about that too. If I had not been holding onto my sanity by a thread, I may have found this to be funny but I didn't.

It was strange to share my story, to rip off the Band-Aid and expose my wound, only to have her pour salt on it.

When the hour was up, Reed was still a no-show. I thanked her and left the session with more questions than when I had arrived. I avoided eye contact with the secretary and didn't stop to make a second appointment.

I felt painfully naive. Why would a woman knowingly allow her husband to cheat on her? Was this really the going trend and, if so, why did I have such a total and complete inability to play along with the script? I felt a prickly anger of indignation rattle in my bones. Fuck that, I thought. Why be married at all if it was just a charade?

I got back to the apartment and looked around at the boxes and the space where Reed's workout equipment had lived. That was what he cared about, his workout equipment. And he left me no option to care for his workout equipment because he had taken it with him. Not that I would have cared for it, it was an Iron Giant, a monstrosity of weights and gadgets that had taken up residence in the middle of our living room. Owen played on it like it was a jungle gym.

I had about twenty-five days until the end of January, and

I still had no idea if I was coming or going. To fill out apartment rental applications, I needed a job. I began looking in the want ads, where I found listings for receptionists, personal assistants, waitresses, and counter help. I knew that beggars shouldn't be choosers, but trying to fit myself into one of these job descriptions felt like squeezing myself into shoes that were too small.

I decided to see if I could channel that deeper wisdom that had greeted me in the parking garage. I sat on the carpeted floor of our apartment while Owen binge-watched *Teletubbies*. I closed my eyes and asked, "How do I find a job that I can do in joy?"

After a few minutes, I was guided to write down everything that I loved to do. Not necessarily things that could pay the bills, just things that made my heart swell.

I wrote down *acting*. Of course this would be my first choice. I loved playing roles and entertaining people. Then I wrote *kids*, which I also had a huge soft spot for. I was the type of person who would cross the street to see a baby; I would regularly stop moms at the mall to compliment their kids. It was weird, but I just liked kids and never met a little one that I didn't want to have a conversation with. Finally, I wrote *parties*. My mother used to tell me, "You never missed a party." She said this in a derogatory way, when she would find me up and hanging out with my older sisters when I should have been in bed. Every time she said it, I thought, that's true, why would anyone want to miss a party?

So that was the list: acting, kids, and parties. I stared down at it, trying to figure out what this was supposed to show me. After a few minutes, I turned back to the newspaper and there before me was an advertisement that I must have overlooked.

It read, "Characters Kids Love is looking for actors to entertain at children's birthday parties." I picked up the phone, dialed the number, and by the end of the call I had an interview for the next day with the promise of working several gigs that very weekend. I would be paid $60.00 a party, plus tips. I could book anywhere between six to eight parties on the weekend. "Basically, we will train you to do magic and face painting and games. Then we will send you out to different events where you will play Power Rangers, and princesses, and Teletubbies," the voice on the phone informed me. "Are you familiar with Teletubbies?" he asked.

"I am afraid I am," I replied.

That whole process was unexpectedly easy, and I was excited by the idea of helping to celebrate kids' birthdays. Still I needed a place to live, and though I had looked through the rental ads, all the options required that I have a huge down payment and proof of employment. So back into stillness I went, hoping to find direction or solutions.

To the soundtrack of *Teletubbies*, I listened but only caught fleeting glimpses of an image. It was of a window with a view of a courtyard, and there was sunlight streaming into what felt like a warm blue room. I had no idea where this room was, but the image came with the feeling of peace. Like a postcard from the future that whispered, "have no fear." Then I heard the words, "Show up, pay attention, tell the truth."

I opened my eyes to the sound of Owen laughing. Show up, pay attention, tell the truth about what? I waited for more insight, but that was it. Show up, pay attention, tell the truth.

I sat on the floor and watched Owen watch the TV and wondered, where was I supposed to show up? What was I supposed to pay attention to? And what did I need to tell the truth about?

I had never before used this type of Guidance, but it began to feel natural and like a smart use of my time. I noticed that as I continued to use the Guidance, it gave me only what I needed to know and nothing more. Like when it came to listing the things I loved, it did not say, "list ten things" just "list what makes you happy." And when it came to the question of where to live, it only gave me an image and a feeling, and yet that amount of information seemed to be enough. Enough to give me the courage to believe that I could stay in LA.

That night, I made arrangements for Owen to go to Laura and Dora's house. They were a mother and daughter that I met at Santa Monica Church. Laura volunteered in the childcare, and we became friends. Owen loved her.

He would stay with them while I went to theater group. I had been a member of the Zeitgeist theater company for the past year. It was an eclectic community of artists, writers, and actors who gathered once a week to work on auditions and writing projects. I used it as a place to share songs and scenes that I had written, and now it would be my poor man's therapy. I showed up that night and attempted to sing a song about my failing marriage. It was sincerely one of the most pathetic songs I had ever written, and I could barely get through it without bawling my eyes out.

Tonight, I will dress up in a smile and over all my pain it will shine through. This is not the last time that my eyes will cry, I know, but it's the last time that my heart breaks over you.

It was cringe-worthy and yet the generous community of artists, who had made the study of the human condition their life's work, applauded my brave vulnerability.

"My husband has left me, and I am looking for a new place to live," I confessed to the entire community. "So, if anyone knows of a place . . ." I shrugged and let it hang there. That confession was a hundred times harder than singing the song, but I did it. It was out there, and then I exited the stage.

Delila, a heavy-set character actress with a sarcastic sense of humor, called me over. I adjusted my Wonderbra straps and made my way to her during the break. "I liked your song, honey," she said. "I wish that I could sing a song like that," she added, "because it would show that I had at least loved someone.

It has been so long since I've had my heart broken that I miss it." Her honesty melted me, and I appreciated that even in my pain, there was someone who could envy my sad and sorry state.

As I sat back down, Skye made her way to the empty seat beside me.

"Bad weather brings us together," she whispered.

This was a phrase I had heard her share often. Her New York childhood exposed her to plenty of bad weather, both authored by mother nature and father time. She cozied up to me and titled towards me, while an older actor took the stage and began a scene from *Angels in America*.

"That song was shit," she said softly. "You do know that, right?"

"Yes, thank you for the clarity."

"Pure trash, you're better than that. But you get a pass due to the current events."

I adjusted my seat and tried to block her out. I hated when she would carry on conversations during other people's work. It felt so entitled and disrespectful.

"Your sucky, shitty situation. It really sucks, he sucks, she sucks, the whole thing sucks," she said matter-of-factly, while staring out at stage.

"Yep." I nodded, "Full on suckfest."

"Look," she continued, "You can't just ask this tribe of pirates to put you up."

I turned back to her, "I am not asking for a handout, I am just looking for a roommate situation or something."

"Right, I know that. But some of these people . . . you just got to be careful."

"I like these people," I shot back in defense, maybe a little too loudly. The older actor cleared his voice and looked our way as we settled back down. After he found his was back into his monologue, she curved back in at me.

"I like these people too, I just think, with Owen, you need to . . . shit."

I looked towards her. "What?" I asked. I could see her struggling, as she gave a deep sigh of resignation.

"Okay, look," she said and turn back slightly. "If you need a place, you know . . ." she paused. "I actually just got into a pretty sweet backhouse in Santa Monica with an extra room. It might be an option for you and Owen for a while, I don't know. It's crazy 'cause I know I don't want to live with you and your rat-faced kid. So I have no idea why I am saying this."

I turned to her. My heart skipped.

"I was hoping for a hot drummer to move in," she said, shaking her head in authentic disappointment. "But I guess I could settle for a single mom." She wrinkled her nose in an exaggerated way, like she had just tasted bad blue cheese. Then she smiled, and I smiled back.

"No promises, just come see it. You guys took me in when I needed a place. This could be some good Karma for me, I can always use some good Karma." She ran her fingers through her thick brown hair in a luxuriously casual way reserved for the childless and free.

It was the first time I heard myself referred to as a single mom in a derogatory way. Even if she was kidding, it felt odd. But I had no time to get hung up, a backhouse in Santa Monica with Skye sounded perfect, and I knew how rare these types of invitations were.

"Are you sure, Skye?" I asked.

"No, no I am not. I am definitely not sure. It's on 23rd street, and we have a yard, and it's actually a pretty cool little home. I rent it from my fat cousin in the front house. She can be a real witch, but you know, I think you might dig it. Stop by tomorrow."

A pretty cool little home sounded exactly like what I was searching for. On my way home from the theatre company, I ran through the rolodex of all my past homes. There had been many. Like a long game of musical chairs, I had bumped and jumped and landed in so many interesting situations. Here I was again, looking for home.

I was born in New Jersey. Placed in my mother's arms, I most likely heard her name before my own.

"Here is your baby, Joan, it's another girl." It was her strong, steady, and warm embrace that taught me what home should feel like. This soft container, with the consistent beat of her heart, soothed me like the ocean.

Entering my first home, I was greeted by a tribe of five feisty girls who had been birthed before me. They gathered around like a strand of twinkle lights. Chirpy voices filling the air, set off by the twirling of dresses and the unceasing questions, and the sweet giggly laughter that came easy and often.

This two-story home on Montague Place was where all my firsts happened, walking, talking, and the rest. It was also where I lived the longest. After sixteen years and the death of my mother, I began moving. Seventeen times over the next ten years, never spending too long in any location. Moving less like a graceful gypsy and more like a savage, a seeker, a thirsty soul.

Seeking a home and harbor and place that could hold my history and handle my truth.

Montague Place was a home of births and deaths, sweaty summers and chilly winters, baptisms, graduations, and proms, and proms, and proms. I spent the first sixteen years of my life watching pretty girls in long dresses pose in front of the azalea bush with tall boys in baby blue tuxedos. It was the home where I was adequate, rocked to sleep with the lullaby of happily ever after.

Montague Place was where my sisters grew like wild front-porch geraniums, filling our home with moxie and music. They would gather up in the attic, their hideout, their bedrooms, their makeshift apartment. My mother called it their opium den and though her cancer prevented her from making her way up all those stairs, it turns out she was not too far off. The rooms were filled with smoke and perfume and stolen lipstick . . . and sea shells used for ashtrays and feather earrings and whispered conversations and hidden shame and guilt and passion and bubble gum wrappers. All set against the soundtrack of train horns and church bells and the siren song of the Good Humor Man that made us search the couch cushions for loose change.

This was the home of Christmas mornings, and late-night Halloweens and Easter egg baskets and Fourth of July fireworks and snow ball fights and long talks on the front stoop.

After my mom died, Montague Place changed, lost it magic, the lights went out. Dad's new wife wanted a different home without all the memories, and so it was sold.

I moved in with my friend Bebe and her divorced mom Patsy. Bebe had an older brother and their home was big enough to get lost in. And I did get lost. In this house, I acquired a sweet addiction to soap operas, thanks to my directionless life. I put on ten pounds thanks to Patsy's great cooking. And I learned about Alcoholics Anonymous thanks to my thirsty ways. Patsy would invite me to my first meeting. But I didn't want to get sober, and Patsy didn't want to be an enabler. So it was time to go.

The next stop was a three-story walk up apartment that I rented with my sister Joan and two other girlfriends. Joan had just gotten her first job working as a social worker, and I was making the rent with modeling jobs. At seventeen and twenty, we decided it was high time that we got our own place so we signed a year lease—and high times it was.

It had not been long since we lost our mother, and we would use this pad to party our pain away. Unfortunately, we could never chase it too far. We furnished our place with thrift shop treasures, sidewalk craft sale artwork, and colorful scarves. It felt like living in the green room of a rock concert complete with the billowy smoke and mirrors and blaring music, thanks to our befriending every musician and drug dealer in a ten-mile radius. Our red-headed roommate, Sadie, would smile at us from across the smoky room and mouth the word "rock stars" over the blaring music. We would bob our heads back at her and respond, "rock stars," which is what we thought we were, even though none of us were in a band, or even played an instrument.

After a year we got tired of the pseudo-rock star life and walking up all those stairs. Joan moved in with her boyfriend, and the band broke up. I rented the third floor of Joan's new house. I had a bedroom and a bathroom and a room for all my shoes—I had a pretty serious collection of shoes at the time. They lined the wall, like characters waiting to be invited out to play.

My next move was to Hoboken, as I moved like a chess pawn making her way across the board of life. Hoboken was a romantic town of brownstones and bars and the perfect place to fall in love, but I didn't. I studied acting by day and served burgers and blue cheese salads by night while dreaming of making it big in show biz.

During a commercial shoot I met Mina. She lived in Stuyvesant Town on the Lower East Side and worked for Barbizon Modeling School. She assured me that I needed to move into the city if I was going to be taken seriously as an actress. Lucky for me she had a room for rent, so I moved in. She had had her boobs done, her legs liposuctioned, her high cheekbones implanted, and her eyeliner and lipstick tattooed on. By the time she was done with all the alterations, she was almost as pretty as when she started. She stood me in front of her mirror and lifted my brows with her fingers and informed me that I would do well with a little lift. I was twenty at the time. She was right about the move though. It did increase my bookings, and I found myself cast in low-budget movies and TV commercials and a short stint on *As The World Turns* as Dee Crain.

During my time in Stuyvesant Town, I did a bit of traveling. I was sent to LA for pilot season by my manager. That's where I first met Skye. We were roommates who loved to ruminate. Soon after that, I ran off to Russia with Alexi, the ticket scalper and Samovars smuggler. We meandered in Turkey and Germany and then to Yugoslavia to see the Blessed Mother and atone for our sins.

After that whirlwind tour, I came back to NY where there was a brief romance and a conception, and a call to my dad to ask him to help move me back to New Jersey to give birth at home. Back to the third-floor apartment where the shoe room would make a lovely little baby room.

And that was when I started dating Reed. Yes, it was interesting timing to say the least. Looking back, I am pretty sure that Reed's attention and flirtation had a lot to do with my new swollen breasts. They must have taken him off guard one day when he blurted out, "Are you wearing new bras?" as he stared at me from across the green room at The Sylvia Leigh Showcase Theatre School on 57th street in Manhattan.

Sylvia Leigh was a well-known acting coach who believed in good articulation, wearing tiaras as an everyday accessory, and me. She believed in me almost as much as she believed in a well-placed tiara, and that was saying something. She let me take free acting classes in exchange for my being a scene partner for her private students. Some of the private clients were attorneys trying to build their chops at public speaking. Then there were a few shy students who were just starting out, and some who were celebrities who flew in from LA for private coaching for movie roles. Reed was none of the above. He was an enthusiastic beginner who had watched his friend rise to recognition and decided, "I want in on that."

He had every reason to suspect stardom. He was tall, dark, and handsome, with an easy smile and a cutting wit. I was definitely attracted to him. But I also never saw us as compatible. He had an intensity about him that bled into everything. I was a go with the flow kind of girl.

Every time I worked as his scene partner, he would invite

me out for drinks or to see a show. I would gently decline, which made him even more interested. I wasn't playing games with him, it was just that I was pregnant and not ready to let the whole world know.

By the time he began questioning my "new bra" situation, I thought I should clue him in. I smiled and shared the news in hopes of clearing the tension.

"I am not really in a position to be dating because I am pregnant," I told him. His eyes grew wide.

"Are you having it?" he asked in shock. I nodded.

"On your own?" he continued as if the thought were inconceivable. I was twenty-four at the time, but I looked much younger for my age, and I am sure he saw me as a child. Which in all honesty, I was. What I thought would have put him off seemed to make him even more enamored of me than ever.

"The biological father was not down with being involved, and I am not down with stringing anyone along for the ride. So yeah, I am doing it on my own."

His eyes softened as he looked down at my swollen breasts that had yet to be eclipsed by a baby bump. "No matter what you say, it will not change how I feel about you, and if you are okay with it, I would like to help you walk through this experience." Those were some of the kindest and sweetest words I could have ever imagined hearing.

Obviously this turn of events, this unorthodox timing was not an optimal springboard to start a relationship. This was not the ordinary courting situation that kicked off your typical romantic comedy, and yet it was surprisingly romantic and fun. Although it did not make much sense to anyone else, Reed and I fell madly and passionately in love with each other.

I loved him more than you would love a man who carries you out of a burning building; I loved him in a way that leaves you shattered and stymied when that love suddenly goes South. I admired and honored and respected him, and at the very foundation of our relationship I liked him. I actually liked him a lot.

We both had a past, we both had our issues, but we just decided that we were both a "yes" to each other and to this new baby. People in our circles would look at us with intrigue. It may have seemed abnormal, but it was our normal, and it worked for us.

I continued to work at the acting studio as a scene partner for celebrities and the shy. I continued working as an actress, mostly as an extra in movies like *Scenes From a Mall* and *Prince of Tides,* to be sure that I kept my SAG insurance, which was golden at the time.

Reed romanced me through the pregnancy. Our untraditional dates took place in Bradley classes or shopping for strollers. He would spend nights with me at my sister's home when he wasn't working.

When my water broke, he rushed in from the city and took off work for the week. He held me during the contractions, feeding me ice chips and encouragements. He was the one to hold Owen through the first night of his life. He confessed to me later that he filled his ears with promises.

"No matter what happens, I will be here for you."

I was overwhelmed by his generosity and level of commitment and love. I felt so blessed and grateful that what I had imagined would be a rough patch turned into something so beautiful.

A few days after Owen was born, Reed begged me to move into his apartment in Sunnyside, Queens. He was tired of making the trek out to Jersey, and he hated not being able to see me and Owen.

I agreed, and our relationship began to bloom. It turned out that Sunnyside, Queens, was not so sunny. I am sure that post-pregnancy is not anyone's optimal hour. But I was also seeing a different side of Reed. He had a pretty dark side that would creep in unexpectedly and rob us of our joy. His intense love and commitment came at a cost; it could just as easily switch to intense rage and jealousy and suspicion. I never knew what would set him off.

I was a pretty transparent person and obviously I had a history. Any mention of other men or previous relationships would bring on a rage that made no sense to me. It was unsettling and confusing, and in the early months of being a new mom, I did my best to avoid confrontations. I was already dealing with lack of sleep and energy. I began to abandon myself so that I could be what he needed.

I would call my sisters after a night of fighting and ask, "Is marriage supposed to be so hard?" But they had no real answers for me.

I was afraid to admit that Reed and I were not doing great, except when it came to fighting. When it came to fighting, we were at the top of our game. Reed was brilliant and used his intellect like a machete, chopping down everything, cutting it all into little pieces and shreds. He loved to discuss and define and debate.

I was terrible at confrontations and conflict. I wanted my rose-colored glasses. I loved stories and sermons and songs. Our communication styles were completely incompatible. He was raised by Italian attorneys and groomed for arguments and accusations. I was raised by Irish gypsies, and groomed for mad rambles and drunken pratfalls.

He was drawn to my lightness, and I was intrigued by his shadows. But that fascination does not a marriage make.

After a year in Sunnyside, Reed began to get the urge to move to LA. I wanted him to be happy and would go where he led. I imagined that if we moved toward the light, we would have an easier time of it. We arrived at a studio apartment in Beverly Hills across from the Four Seasons on the day of the Rodney King riots. We were met with more turmoil than we had left.

Our relationship became rough and strained and strange. And home? Home was a distant memory.

Soon, the studio apartment would become too small. Owen needed a place to roam, and so we moved to a three-bedroom apartment in Beverly Hills adjacent on Wooster place. We rented the extra bedroom to Skye after she moved back to LA from New York. It was great having her around. She would take Owen to the mall and made sure his first full sentence was, "Can I go to the Beverly Center and get a cappuccino?"

This is where Owen would learn the alphabet, and then words, and then he would learn to talk. He would absorb all the words that we said and regurgitate them back at us. Donuts and dinosaurs and, of course, divorce. This was the home where I found the love letter in the armrest, and the rest is history.

Here I was once again, looking for home. After leaving my first home on Montague Place, all the other ones were more like hostels than home. I was longing for a place to land, to heal and hibernate. A place where Owen would feel safe and happy.

Since moving from New York, I had dreamed of living closer to the beach, and now was the time to make that happen. I found Skye's address and made my way to the little backhouse, pushing open the gate and entering into a secret garden. I moved along the side yard to the back porch with the view of the swing set. The whole scene was drenched in sunlight and salty sea air. Skye met me at the door with a flower in her hair and a paint-brush in her teeth.

She wiped her paint-smeared hands on her jeans and pulled the brush from her lips like it was a long cigarette. "Come in!"

This enchanted little fairy shack, sporting sparkle paint on the ceiling, hardwood floors, a little front porch, and a cast of lovable eccentrics that came right out of the irregular bin. I felt as though I fit right in.

The best part was that Laura and Dora lived a few blocks away. Dora had raised Laura as a single mother, and when I shared with them the new situation, they were very sympathetic. "Anytime you need help, we will be here," they both pledged. "We are here for you both anytime. We love that baby boy. He is our good boy."

There is nothing like having someone love your kid the way you love him. I can't tell you how much that support meant to me at that time. Aside from Skye, I had no family in the area. They were as close to family as I had in Santa Monica, and now I had the possibility of living a few blocks away from them.

Skye and I stood in the living room under the sparkle ceiling as we struck up an agreement.

"This is it," she said, holding her hands out like a game show host.

There was an old kitchen table with a diverse assortment of chairs, a television resting on a milk crate, and in the corner there was an old fashioned beauty salon chair with a hair dryer attachment.

"Are you doing hair these days?" I asked.

"I've been thinking about it. I won that in a poker game. And don't knock it till you try it."

"Okay." I replied.

"So, what do you think?" she asked.

"I think I am in love."

"How about the rent?"

"I am good for it."

"I know you are. I need eight hundred for your end of the deposit."

I took the eight hundred bucks from my pocket. Eight hundred was all I had, and for now, it was all I needed. I handed her my life savings, and we walked out to the front porch and watched Owen hang upside down from the swings.

"I should let you know about the bathroom," she said, while tucking the money in her back pocket.

"What about the bathroom?" I asked.

"It's just really small. I mean totally doable, but it's just that you kind of have to sit sideways."

"Seriously?"

"The bath comes up on one side and the sink comes out on the other, and you sort of need to shoehorn your ass in there and lean your knees to one side. It's not a major thing."

"Okay." I nodded. "Beggars can't be choosers I guess."

Skye grew up with four other siblings in a two-bedroom apartment in New York. The one time I visited her there, they had a toy mountain in the middle of their living room. Not a hill or a dune or a knoll but a full-on toy mountain that they were all very proud of. So I knew she was used to living in unconventional places in offbeat ways. Of course she had a home where you needed to sit side saddle in the loo.

Almost instantly, the dread of the future began to fade. Not completely of course, but something huge was lifted and the feeling was confirmed by the most enchanting sign.

As I began to move my boxes into the back house, I saw the sign the very first time I looked down to take the steps up the backstairs to the main door. On the cement step, I saw that someone had engraved a name. I didn't have to look too close to read it. It was right out there in the open waiting for me to find it. It was the name, Joan, my mother's name.

I put down the bags that I had been carrying and sat on the stoop, staring at the letters as I traced them with my finger. J-O-A-N. It was a sign when I needed it most. I was home.

So this was it. This is what could happen when you showed up, told the truth, and paid attention.

— TOOL —

Signs and symbols

Signs and symbols are all around us, it is up to us to pay attention to them. They are the secret language of the heart.

We spend too many hours seducing the problem, romanticizing the issue, and entertaining the pain. It can leave us drained and depressed. Looking up and looking out for signs is a great way to create another conversation with your Divine.

God holds no investment in your struggle but giving up the struggle can sometimes feel as uncomfortable as giving up air. Why? Because we have built elaborate temples to our broken stories and dismantling these temples means dismantling the very idea of who we are. Our blind spots are woven through our identities, and no one wants to come undone.

— DO THIS —

As you move through this book, take a moment to pick a sign that will remind you that you are on course with your optimal outcome. Ask your Divine to sprinkle your path with signs and symbols.

Practice the art of paying attention and expecting signs, symbols, and synchronicities. The more you expect them, the more you celebrate them, the more you will find them. The Divine is sending you love letters all day long. If you ask for signs, She will come.

She will come to you in sunsets and rain and the sticky whisper of a child. She will greet you in the warmth of the coffee cup, a song on the radio, and school girls singing on the back of the bus. She is there in the silent hours of night. Standing witness as you wash the dishes and blow dry your hair and drive your car. It might surprise you at first. You might think, I did not know I could find the Divine in the laughter of a stranger or a spoonful of lentil soup. But She is there, and if you pay attention, you will have your holy communions with Her in every hour and every breath. Her company will cause you to smile and find peace, and you will return to Her again and again as a faithful little bin diver.

Chapter 3

Take Your Time

Child of God, you were created to create the good,
the beautiful and the holy. Do not forget this.
—*A Course in Miracles*

I knew that I was responsible for the shape that my life was in. I knew that I had gotten not what I had deserved, but what I had thought that I deserved. My best thinking had gotten me to this place. So there was obviously a problem with my best thinking.

My whole head space was definitely jacked, because as crazy as it sounds I was still holding out hope that Reed and I would patch things up. I know . . . in what strange alternative universe did that even make sense? I would cry, coax, cajole, beg, bargain, and plead. I was in deep denial and desperation. Plus, I seemed to have a high tolerance for pain.

Once a week, on Saturday, Reed would come by to pick up Owen. This gave me the chance to spend the day entertaining little birthday princesses. The first couple of weeks that he came,

I watched myself awkwardly try to start up pathetic conversations about our possible reconciliation. You would have thought that the sexy Cinderella or Princess Jasmine costume would have worked in my favor. Nope. Each visit, he would find a new and more degrading way of shooting me down. It was like Disney Princess Whack-A-Mole. So that was fun.

Then he would take Owen off to spend the day with Miss Universe in her fancy house with rich people food. At least that was how Owen explained it when he got home, and yes, I did bribe him for details. So that was a new low.

After each Saturday encounter with Reed, I would drive myself around LA dressed as a weeping clown or a sad Snow White. Good times! Outside the homes, I would blow my nose, re-apply my make-up, and make my merry way into the party to share fairytales about happily-ever-after with little girls.

It took some time to get acclimated. Starting over in a new neighborhood where I knew no one was rough, and every so often I would find myself in the fetal position on the very small bathroom floor. But then I would get up and show up to the next thing. I began to understand and appreciate the idea of "show up, pay attention, tell the truth." I had not mastered it, but I did appreciate it. I used it as a mantra, especially when I was feeling like I just wanted to pack it in.

It's astounding to think that strength is the thing that you meet in your weakest moment. My personal ground zero was the foundation for huge growth.

When I look back at those days that stumbled in after Miss Universe's boyfriend moved out of my life, I am amazed by the little powerhouse that I became. I didn't know I had it in me.

No one can really teach you how exit a car crash, in the same way that no one likes to talk about divorce at a wedding. No one tells you how to prepare for devastation. You can't really experience your own strength from the stories of others. It's not until your feet hit the fire that you learn how to dance.

Showing up and paying attention was doable. But the truth telling part was territory that I had no map for. The more I ventured into this new terrain, the more I realized how horrible I was at actually telling the truth. Like really fucking bad. I am not sure if I would have known the truth if it bit me on the ass. All my allegiances were wrapped in misinformed and unquestioned agreements that held no real weight or water. I was supposed to stay married. I kept my wedding band on, and told my family that Reed and I were just working things out. This was not even close to the truth, but I just could not muster the courage to break the news to them. "We're just going through a rough patch," I would tell them. Because the idea of saying, he is fucking Miss Universe was not even something I was willing to admit to myself.

So I wore my wedding band, and spoke about "my husband", and pretended that this thing was just a phase. Inside I felt as though the filing cabinets that held all my beliefs had just been dumped out on the floor. I rummaged through the laws and loyalties that had formed my thought system. I was shocked at how archaic and limiting they were. This fresh canvas had given me a gift that few get; the gift of questioning everything. I was being called to reach down, remember, retrieve, and resurrect the truth. As poetic as all that sounds, it was not easy. In fact, to tell you the truth, it sucked.

Nevertheless, this was my new normal. Despite the pain and awkwardness of it all, I had a slight understanding that one day I would look back on all of this and laugh.

But until that comical transformation happened, I needed to keep putting one foot in front of the other and walk in the real world, amongst the mortals. In so doing, I began to grow an appreciation for how brave we all are to attempt to navigate real life with its jagged scripts, bad lighting, and interesting plot twists.

One such plot twist came a month into my living in Santa Monica. My car got hit by a couple that was plowing down the alley behind my house. Not expecting me to pull into the cross-way, they crashed into my beautiful, clunky, old Falcon. They were hugely apologetic, making sure I was okay, and offered to pay for the crunched fender. "If we could avoid going through the insurance company, that would be great," they added.

I got a couple estimates and sent them over to the email address on their business card. When I went to pick up the check from their office, I was met with the most unsettling sight.

I stepped into the waiting room and found myself surrounded by a million images of pretty girls in suits and sashes smiling back at me with Stepford eyes, blood red lips, and miles of cleavage. I must have looked like I was going to pass out. It turned out that they ran the Miss America Pageant.

"Are you okay?" the woman asked.

"Oh yeah, it's just that I didn't know that you ran the Miss America Pageant." And then I blurted out, "My husband is with Miss Universe."

"Oh really? What does he do for them?" she asked.

"Well, I guess I should say my former husband," I stammered. "And it's not really *what* he does . . . but *who?* I mean. He is *with* Miss Universe, as in dating." I am pretty sure that this was the first time I had to explain the situation to a stranger outside of the "helpful" therapist in Beverly Hills. It felt cruel that God would play such a joke on me, but it was such a specific scenario that I had to pay attention to it. It was like God was saying, "Can you hear me now?"

Would it take this twisted wake up call to get me to realize that he had moved on? Did I really need to be side-swiped to get my attention and begin to face and speak the truth? He had left me, and he was not coming back.

I had begged, bargained, and pleaded my way back into our marriage. I had promised to work on myself. I would be better. I would go to marriage counseling. I would go to the moon. I did not want to walk away from my marriage without a fight. But he was gone. And speaking it aloud against the backdrop of beauty queens witnessing my confession made it all the more real. He is with Miss Universe. He is my former husband. He is gone.

The woman's face went flat, and the room filled with a silent sorrow. Suddenly we were not strangers, we were two people with a deeper appreciation of our human condition. I took a breath and bit my lip and tried to force a smile. My words seemed to echo off the walls, and in the silence, I also heard the woman whisper, "I am sorry." She signed her name and then handed me the envelope, and I left. I am pretty sure she added an extra hundred dollars to the check.

Between the move, and the stress, and lack of appetite, I lost ten pounds that I did not have to lose. And then I did the one thing that they tell you not to do, I cut all my hair off. Not all of it, but most of it. I went from Julia Roberts to Ellen DeGeneres, and you know what? They are right on the money with this one. Cutting all your hair off does not make anything better. But there you have it, live and learn.

With the new haircut and the extra flat chest, I began looking like a twelve year old boy, making it all the more painful when Miss Universe would come with Reed to do the hand off. It did not matter if we were at a park or a soccer game or a cemetery, she had a standard outfit, that came in different colors like a Barbie doll. It was high heels, mini skirt, and a tight top. Her natural accessories of impossibly long legs, ridiculous rack, and incredible hair made me want to date her too. I mean come on! It was hard not to stare at her as she gracefully navigated the soccer field in *high heels!* It was like a magic show. How was she doing that? Did beauty queens have super powers?

Whenever I saw Miss Universe coming, I longed for a baseball cap or a pair of dark sunglasses. I felt so exposed around her, like every emotion was playing across my face and I couldn't stop it. I wished I was taller, prettier, cooler, and at the same time, invisible.

The new short hair did help out with the quick changes that I needed to implement in the car between parties as I went from the Little Mermaid to Barbie to Belle. I felt like a snake oil salesman showing up to entertain the birthday girls with stories of handsome princes and romance and true love. I did my best to debunk it.

They would often ask me, "Belle, where is the Beast?" Or "Pocahontas, where is John Smith?"

"Oh he is at home cooking me dinner," I would say with a wink to the mom who was usually wringing her hands with worry that I would be found out as "a fraud." They had just plunked down two-hundred dollars to give their kid a party to remember with their favorite princess. I had best be delightful and keep the magic alive.

In earnest, I wanted to take each of those little cherubs aside and say, "Get yourself some marriage insurance, because sometimes the prince can turn back into a toad. But you didn't hear that from me." However, since the tip was a main part of my income, I held my tongue.

Some nights, I would wake myself up screaming Reed's name. I thought that was something that only happened in movies. I felt like I was running just to keep up, and even though we were no longer married, it seemed like Reed could still cause havoc in my life. He could still say jump, and I would take flight. I had a real hard time including myself in the equation.

"You just need to find your footing. You're giving away your power," Skye insisted one day while licking and rolling her lips as she flicked her cigarette into our side yard. She had come out to the back porch in boy shorts and a bathing suit top to get some sun and steal candies from me as I filled the piñatas for my parties.

"How does this sound?" she asked, reading off a slip of paper. "Skye is a writer, actor, bartending yoga enthusiast who also does stand up." She beamed. "It's my bio for the next show."

"You don't do stand up," I suggested.

"Well, not yet," she corrected. Then she leaned and puckered her lips. She had perfected the popular duck lip smirk and intense eye gaze that had secured her a few national commercials. The combination of her low-brow humor, generous life advice, and ability to give good face was the secret sauce that filled her tip jar. She had recently attended some motivational mindset meetings, and whether I liked it or not, I would be one of her guinea pigs. Honestly, I welcomed all the help I could get.

"You need to retrace your tracks and reclaim your power and figure out how you got here. You need to locate where you left your dharma." She took a deep breath, leaned in, and asked, "So how did you get here?" I had grown accustomed to her colorful vocabulary and Tony Robbins technique. I wanted to tell her that I literally moved myself in my convertible Ford Falcon, packing boxes and boxes into the backseat and trunk by myself. I wanted to tell her about how my "wasband" had not lifted a fucking hand, so it took me several trips from Beverly Hills to Santa Monica with Owen strapped into his car seat, riding shotgun. I wanted to tell her how Reed had not just left me, but he left everything except his workout equipment. And how staring at the indentation that it left our carpeted floor made my mind swirl. I wanted to tell her of the complete amputation that came with the precision of a guillotine. And how shocked I was by all the ways I had gotten it wrong.

I am not sure what I had expected. I had never separated

before, so I had imagined that we would go through our things together, sort out all the stuff, the trinkets and treasures that you compile over the duration of a relationship. But he had gone off script and washed his hands of all of it, not a picture, not a pillow, not even a play toy for Owen to have when he went to his house. He did, however, gladly carry the weight of a workout machine in a shopping cart. These were the thoughts that plagued me. The questions that I knew I would never get answers for. These were the hot topics that I could not let go of, even if they were burning my hands off.

I wanted to tell Skye about the packing and the pain and the position of the therapist who suggested that I just go along to get along. But I didn't because I had a feeling Skye was pressing me for something deeper. "How did you get here?" she asked again. "And how are you going to take your power back?"

The questions made me queasy. I had little patience for solutions. Not when I could tell her stories of what an A-hole my "wasband" was. "He was most likely cheating on me the whole time," I moaned trying to redirect the subject.

"Oh yeah, most definitely," she added with no emotional investment, just more intense eye gazing. It was extremely uncomfortable.

"Okay!" I conceded. How did I get here? How had I so seamlessly slipped into such a mentally abusive relationship? How had I not seen the forest for the trees? How could I have been so stupid?

Skye lifted Owen's half-eaten PB&J to her mouth and took a deep bite.

"You're not stupid," she finally offered after swallowing the rest of his sandwich. "You're bad with boundaries. You let him run the show and cast you as an extra," she clarified as she unwrapped a Tootsie Roll and popped into her mouth. God that hurt.

She grinned a chocolatey smile at her own cleverness, and I could tell that bit was going to end up in her stand-up routine.

"The cure-all is creativity," she continued. "you got to stay creative. If your brain gets bored, you'll start taking all kinds of wrong turns. Trust me!" she said and flicked the candy wrapper at my face for emphasis.

"Stay creative or your boredom will exhaust you and make you do the kind of stuff that could land you in the big house." She reached down and scratched the Hello Kitty tattoo on the back of her calf, and I trusted that she knew what she was talking about.

"I do want my power back," I confessed, like Dorothy asking Glinda for a ticket to Kansas. I reached for the other half of Owen's neglected sandwich.

"Well, you gotta get your groove back and stop focusing on him. And if he asks you for anything, don't answer him right away. Tell him you have to think about it and make him wait for the answer."

"Why would I do that?" I asked.

"Because he's got you trained like a monkey. He speaks, and you drop everything, and you end up making all kinds of decisions that you regret. Make him wait," she repeated. "You can take your sweet ass time."

I was uncomfortable with her summation of me. But she was right. I was a bit of a trained monkey.

As if she could read my mind, she continued, "Trust me, no matter what he asks, make him wait at least twenty-four hours. That will get your power back." She pulled a drag from her cigarette, and then added, "Also, you should be having lots of sex right about now."

I shook my head, "I am not going to be having lots of sex. I have a kid and I am not ready and—"

She stopped me. "Fine!" She conceded while grabbing a handful of Smarties.

"Maybe I am the one who needs the sex," she laughed. "But trust me, Maureen, you got serious root chakra issues, and you gotta cut the cords." She pointed her cigarette at me and narrowed her eyes. "Anyone can see that." Then she sat for a while, sucking the candy from her teeth and blowing smoke rings at the sky. When she was done, she turned back to me.

"Your root chakra is all about stability and your family of origin. You got to get in touch with your roots," she said while playfully patting her crotch. I shook my head and laughed.

"It's most likely that you're codependent, and you need to get your spider energy back.

"I'm sorry—spider energy?"

"Yes, the spider knows her worth. That's why she scares the crap out of people. She is the solo artist, creatrix of her life who makes her living from her craftiness. She just weaves her kick-ass web and waits for life to deliver itself to her. She carries her home with her and she is not afraid to be visible. Sitting right out there in the middle of her artistry like a gangster."

"So I need spider energy?"

"You, my dear, are efforting too much." I nodded and she continued on. ·

"Also I have some Bergamot oil for you which works for protection, or was it prosperity? Maybe both actually now that I think about it. And here." She twisted a ring from her finger and handed it to me. "Wear this, it's rose quartz, good for self-love" She leaned her head to one side and smiled at me, as if I was a painting that she was finally satisfied with. Then, just for good measure, she added, "And you should probably get your ass in a yoga class."

She ticked these things off like a witch doctor doling out prescriptions. I nodded, assuring her with my eyes that I was listening. I did not really understand most of what that she was saying, but I liked it a lot more than the suggestion of, "just accept he has a girlfriend."

She stood and wiped the crumbs from her mouth with the back of her tattooed hand, before making her way back inside. First thing I needed to find out was, what the hell was a root chakra?

The yoga studio was down the block from Owen's preschool. I could drop him off and then drive my sweet Ford Falcon a few more blocks to the yoga studio. The studio was run by Bryan Kest, who taught the class topless. The combination of his beautiful body and his Zen disposition rattled me.

His class was filled with young beautiful Hollywood hopefuls laying their limbs out on thin yoga mats as Bryan gently guided us through foreign poses. Stretching us into pretzels and then soothing us with words and wisdom about relaxing and going with the flow and owning your space. It felt intoxicating and also like he was speaking in tongues. Again, I understood none of it and yet loved every bit. Every sound and syllable a sacred treasure that dripped into my thirsty soul. It was his New York accent that sealed the deal and made me feel safe. For the next year, I went religiously to the chapel of Bryan Kest and slowly but consistently re-carved myself and rewired my brain. I had no idea what I was doing, but I just kept going back and showing up and twisting and bending and stretching and then, my favorite pose, savasana, corpse pose.

At the end of every class for that magical year, I would find myself wrung out and laid to rest in corpse pose. And without fail my tears would come and mix with my sweat and run down the sides of my face and into my ears, and I would drop into a second or two of peace that could carry me through to the next class. And it was good.

This extra hour of stillness a day gave me the ability to pay attention to my own truth and listen still deeper to my Divine.

Instead of coming to conversations fractured like a puppet on the strings of everyone else's plans and desires, I became slightly detached from all my thinking. Then one day without apologies, or excuses, or explanation I began to make Reed wait before responding to his questions and requests. It didn't seem like it would be that big a deal and so it was startling how impactful it was.

"Let me think about that and I'll get back to you" was a script that seemed so alien. Who was I to take my time and contemplate? Who was I to include myself and my feelings into the equation? Who was I to allow myself to take the time to think things through?

I was so used to knee-jerk responses inspired by fear. But here I was crafting a new script for myself that gave me the strength to deliver an honest and conscious "yes" or "no."

So what if my "decision maker" had gotten hijacked in the past? I could choose again. I could check in with my own authority, ask for what I needed, and reject what I did not want. I no longer had to settle for having my desires trampled by the wishes and wills of others.

The more time I spent in silence, the more distance I got from Reed, and the more that I began including myself in the decisions, the more I came to realize how codependent I had been. It was not a light switch, it was a process. A new dance that I was learning the steps to, and most of the time it felt like I was patting my head and rubbing my belly and literally retraining my brain.

Every time I reverted to my old ways, I saw how right Skye was. Reed would say jump, and up I would leap, not even waiting to ask, "how high."

I was getting to see that I was a girl who couldn't say "no." It caused me so much discomfort and guilt. But at least now I was learning, or rather, un-learning. Though it was not easy. Especially when it came to making spaghetti. That was actually what did it. That was what caused me to shut down the whole show, spaghetti.

In the theatre company, I was cast in a scene where I played a woman in the beginnings of a romantic relationship. The other actor was a great guy named Drew. He was handsome, with honest eyes and a sharp sense of humor. We had become friends and he was very sympathetic to my recent turn of events. We shared relationship war stories. Since I did not live far from the theater, we would meet at my house to rehearse and share a meal before group. I could tell that if I was open, it would have been way more than that. I was also very invested in not hurting his feelings. It sounds pedestrian, but my thinking went like this: *he likes me, so I should like him back, to the same degree that he likes me, or else I am not a nice or kind person.* I really wanted to be a nice and kind person. That was the deck I was dealing with. It had no queens, only extra jokers.

One day after we were done with our scene, I started making spaghetti while he stood behind me, slightly breathing down my neck.

"You're not gonna rinse the pasta?" he asked.

"No." I replied, and then for some strange reason he went on a short monologue about how you "needed" to rinse that pasta. Pulling up all sorts of substantial facts about starch and health, he had a degree of passion around pasta rinsing that made me feel uncomfortable. It was the same discomfort that I felt with Reed, but I never addressed. The same discomfort that I had just decided to live with. But for some reason, maybe because of all the yoga and self-assessments that I was doing, I stopped, turned to him and said, "No. I don't rinse the pasta, and no matter what evidence you have to show for the pros of pasta rinsing, I still will not rinse the pasta. Not because I am right, and you are wrong, but because I simply don't want to rinse the fucking pasta. So if that is going to fuck you up, then you're gonna want to skip this meal."

It was that moment that I knew, I could not be in a relationship. I knew the outburst was not about Drew, or Reed or pasta—it was about me finding my voice and finding a way to speak it without setting a fire.

In the moment, I just wanted to eat the fucking pasta, and I didn't want to have to deal with anyone telling me how to do it. And if I should die from over consumption of starch, I had come to the aha awareness that I would die happy. It was not a revolutionary spiritual awakening. It was just your average, run of the mill moment, but it ushered in my authentic voice. I stood in that moment as he stared back at me with his chin on the floor, and I felt a rush of surprised appreciation. Like running into an old friend in an unexpected place. The friend was my truth and the place was my kitchen and the catalyst was spaghetti, and I gotta tell you that that pasta was, to this day, the tastiest that I have ever devoured.

The more my voice came back, the more I found myself laughing. That was a welcomed sound. "Laughter is the best revenge," Skye reminded me that February 1st, after I handed her my rent check. "It's national freedom day. The 13th amendment was signed outlawing slavery!" She lifted a glass of wine and toasted in my direction.

"To freedom." I toasted back.

We spent the night warming the stoop with a case of sparklers and a couple bottles of wine and we freckled the night with laughter.

It was a good night, but in truth my recovery was not always so graceful. Most times it was like watching a drunk open a door with a corkscrew.

The thing about setting boundaries is that, at first, it felt like I was setting fire to things. I felt like I needed a blow torch instead of a match because in the past my boundaries were not always respected.

I obviously had a distrust of boundaries. My truth having

been silenced, trampled, and trespassed, I had lost faith in the weight of my words. I had somehow allowed my words to be whittled down by the world until my "no" looked like a "yes." I was guilt's little bitch. I wanted everyone to like me and would do whatever it took to make that happen. I felt pulled, fractured, thin, unproductive, and confused. I was aware that I was spinning, wasting a ton of energy and not getting anywhere. I needed to find another way of being if I were to survive. Drastic times called for drastic measures.

So it was over a plate of spaghetti that I decided I needed to make a big change, a change that I needed to announce to the world. I was going to have a boundary even if it killed me.

Obviously, my issues were tied up in how I saw myself in relationship to others. How I had allowed myself to be defined by other's thoughts and expectations. The only way to clear a path to my own truth was to unplug completely. I went the way of the monks and nuns and declared my one year of celibacy, a complete sabbatical from dating.

This proclamation made Skye fear for my sanity. She sat at the kitchen table, staring back at me with a bewildered expression as Owen devoured his bowl of cereal.

"Why? I don't get it, what good will that do? Are you some kind of sex Nazi?" she asked incredulously.

"No, I am doing this for me, because I want to get to know myself. All that love, relationships, all of it . . . I just can't. It's too much energy that I don't have to spend. It's a game that I don't know how to play, so I am just benching myself."

"Sounds like you're putting yourself in the penalty box." She smirked while grabbing a handful of Captain Crunch and leaning back against the wall.

"I just know myself. One kiss and it's 'I love you' and one

'I love you' becomes 'I *am* you.' Then I rent out my head to what you think of me and *if* you think of me, and I just don't have that space to give."

"But a year?" she countered.

"A year at least," I replied. It was like I was in a hot air balloon and cutting the sandbags that weighed me down. I was speaking my truth. It felt clean like fresh spring water. I could feel it, and I was learning to speak it and defend it even if it did not make sense to anyone else.

I had gotten into this position and I would get myself back out. More than accepting the fact that Reed left me, I had to accept that I had left myself. I had left myself in every relationship, surrendered my "me" for our "we." It happened in every situation. A fast and unconscious fade that I seemed to have little control over. The only hope was to step away and recalibrate my being.

One year of no mixing, merging, or melding with the opposite sex. Okay, during the twelve months, which actually turned into eleven, (but we will get to that) there were a few close calls with a very handy and hot yoga instructor. But I was so off kilter that I was not really sure if his "adjustments" were actually just "adjustments" or if they were advances. Either way, it didn't matter. I was sticking to my plan. Sure, sex and romance were tempting. I had not been a free agent in four years. A new relationship seemed like just the thing to distract me from the pain, but I stayed the course and stuck to my guns. Romantic relationships were not on the menu. My trust had been severed and seared. I was raw in an almost untouchable way.

It was not too hard to stick to the "no man plan." After you've been tragically tossed from a the carnival ride, there is no real rush to get back in line for another round.

That night I sat on my stoop, looked out at the night skies and made a promise, a vow not so much to my God or my guide, but just to myself.

I promised to give myself a year. A year of doing things

differently, of not looking for someone to save me. A year of savoring myself. And as if on cue, I heard Bruce Springsteen croon at me from a passing car, warning me not to waste my summer, because a savior was not about to rise from these streets. I sighed and smiled. This time I would save myself. Before I fell in love with anyone else ever again, I would attempt to fall in love with myself. I needed to take down the old dusty cobwebs and weave something new from scratch.

This clean slate was both terrifying and liberating. Looking down at my son as he slept in that little red bed jammed into my walk-in closet, I made a promise to him too. As much as I craved it, the fetal position was no longer an option. As weighted as my feet felt, as heavy as my heart was, I would step forward, and I would do it on my own. One link at a time, one day at a time, weaving a new life of my own design. I would give up being rescued and attempt a resurrection.

⟶ TOOL ⟶

Take your time clear your space

In order to grow, you have to let go of all that you are and all that you know. There are not too many things that we have dominion over, but we are responsible for our time and space. Which is surprising, given that we live in cluttered corners with congested calendars. If we are not paying attention, we could develop an addiction to the high of rushing and getting and filling the space. Pushing things into form before we are really ready. Filling seats and clicking boxes to beat the clock. There is nothing beautiful about being busy. It's time to take back our power, savor the simplicity. From this blank canvas, we can take our time to contemplate and create a life that is in alignment with our most authentic being.

⟶ DO THIS ⟶

Be still. Carve out some open space and meditation breaks. Unplug yourself from the mad merry-go-round of the world. Trust me—you can get back on whenever you like. Be radical about owning your time and space. Life has a way of trying to make us her bitch. Rip a page from my no-fail happiness plan: if you can't do it in peace, don't do it. I promise the world will not fall apart. You think you need to be everywhere and do everything, but the more you say no, the more life will do the heavy lifting in the most magical ways.

Take an assessment of all the areas of your life and clear away anything that is not serving you. Give yourself a break from toxic relationships. Continue to get comfortable with the open space and silent hours. Get mindful in the mundane, settled in the simple. And while you take your next small steps, hold a place of knowing that the Divine has got designs on your future. For now, leave tomorrow to the more competent hands of God and commit to romancing the peaceful pace of life. You got this.

Chapter 4

You Have Greatness
Within You

Nothing real can be threatened. Nothing unreal exists.
Herein lies that peace of God.
—*A Couse in Miracles*

I sat courtside that year in regards to romance. Though being out of the game did not preclude me from falling in love, because I did. I fell madly and deeply in love with creating. I had this awesome little backhouse that I filled with refurbished yard sale finds, a ton of throw pillows and, of course, a blessed mother statue, and Venus on a half shell for the garden. I started to entertain again and host parties. I strung twinkle lights and began cooking and painting and writing more than ever.

I fell head over heels in love with my craft as an actress. The interesting thing was that instead of sinking, as Reed had predicted, I was thriving, and no one was more surprised than me. Thanks to the easily available emotions, due to the recent heartbreak, and the loss of weight, I began booking work like crazy. Shooting national commercials and TV shows, making my own money, paying my own bills, and not having to answer to anyone.

I soon realized that if I did my own parties, I would get to keep a bigger share of the money. So I started my own party entertainment company called Princess Parties. Turns out you can cover a lot of miles when you are flying solo. I didn't always feel like a badass. Most of the time, I felt like I was just doing my best to put another day behind me where I didn't end up raising my son under a highway overpass and pushing a shopping cart. I decided to channel all my angst and anger into the characters that I was playing. It was a poor man's therapy, but weirdly it worked.

I continued to connect with my inner teacher, and I made an art out of paying attention to signs and symbols. Owen and I would make a game out of it.

"Today, I will see a rainbow."

"Today, I will see a tiger."

Once Owen said, "I will see a man with a bird on his head." I thought that sign was a little specific but didn't say anything.

Later that day, we were at a park when the Good Humor Man arrived. We went running over and placed our order.

"Look, Mom." Owen said and pointed at the man's hat. Sure enough, there was a blue jay on the man's head.

I spent most nights doing theatre. I got cast in play after play through the theatre company, and the theatre became our second home. Owen and I would grab some fast food for dinner, and then go to the theatre. I would perform on stage, while Owen would hang out backstage amidst the make-up and musings of the cast. Honestly, I am not sure if it was the optimal way to raise a kid, but it was me doing the best I could under the circumstances.

It was hard to know how much to share with Owen, how to explain the new situation, and when to just pretend that it was all normal. He was such a serious little kid to begin with, but as a baby, I used to call him my little old man. He would look around at the world with such a contemplative gaze as if to say, "How did I get here? And what the hell is this place?"

It was no surprise that he grew into a curious kid. Once he learned to talk, all the questions and contemplations that had sat on his face as a baby now had a vehicle for expression. He wanted to know about everything. "How does the sun come up? Where does it come from? Where does it go at nighttime? And where does the moon live?"

"Where does the moon live?" His questions made me sit up. His questions fed my soul. I'd write all his wonders down in his baby book. It was like having a traveling poet with me at all times.

"Mommy, the moon is following us," he whispered one night from his car seat as we drove over Mulholland drive. His helium voice, his beautiful innocent observations transformed my world into something sacred.

During the separation, he seemed to slip back into his quieter ways. He seemed to get older faster. He still had his helium voice, but he asked harder questions; ones that I didn't have all the answers to.

"Why are we moving? Where is my dad? When is he coming back? Why did he forget about me?"

I did my best, to tell him a gentle version of the truth. "We are just taking some time to be apart, we are just figuring out how to play well together." I was pretty deep in single parent-survival mode. I made up for the guilt by buying him stuff—like lots of stuff. This was not a great solution, but it was the price I was willing to pay to see my kid happy.

I read every divorce book I could get my hands on, but most of them felt like they were written by robots. The helpful list of well crafted and choreographed steps suggested as a way to dance your way through divorce looked nothing like the spastic mosh pit simulated by myself and Reed. I circled and highlighted all the ways we were failing.

Still, I kept reading. Several of the books said that your child will not mourn until they see the parent who is experiencing the most grief begin to show signs of healing. It was amazing to think that kids actually put off their own grief process until their mom or dad seem stable again. I stayed on the lookout for that moment; vigilant for when he would be comfortable enough to share his sadness. Then when it came, I was not actually ready.

It showed up one day while I was driving Owen to school.

"Mom, why is this happening?" It was so soft and casual, that at first I didn't recognize it for what it was.

"Why is what happening?"

"Why is this happening?" he asked again, and it was this second time that got my attention. There was a brief silence, and he asked it a third time, along with little huffs and swallowed sobs.

"You and dad, and us living in two different houses? Why don't I get to see my dad all that much?"

Here it was. My heart went to the floor. I looked over at his normally curious blue-sky face, but on that day, it was covered with storm clouds. If you've ever been to this barbwire, broken-down moment, you know first-hand the grace it takes to walk through these landmines. Witnessing your kid's sorrow that's caused from your own failed relationship is a particularly hot spot in hell. That arrow pierces you right in the jugular.

I pulled the car over, summoning my strength as I navigated the sudden flood of pure uncut rage that coursed through my body. All the anger that I had withheld for Reed and Miss Universe, that I had attempted to tuck away, now came like a swarm of bees pricking me on every inch of my body.

Seeing my child suffer brought forth my mother bear, and I wanted to take down the world. But that was not what this moment was about. This moment was about being there for my son. It's a strange and complex moment when all your assets are suddenly flying out the window, but you know you need to hold it all together. To navigate the moment with hair-pin precision and super-human control. It's not the type of thing you would wish on anyone. I turned my body to look at him.

"Owen, it has nothing to do with you. It's not your fault. You didn't cause it, and sometimes some things are not meant to last forever." I could see my explanations were falling like raindrops against a window of pain. I was getting nowhere.

I sat back and looked out at the busy morning, bustling with business people walking to work, moms with Starbucks and strollers, high school kids and homeless people, coming and going on Wilshire. Here we were in the tapestry of life, just two little threads of this bigger picture, and I had to figure out how to help him get untwisted. How to get him to see his connection to it all and show him that he was not alone. I had to explain why this terrible, horrible, very bad thing was happening to him.

I remembered the story that my father told me when my mom was dying, and my own heart was being smashed. I didn't understand why it was happening, or how I would ever survive it.

I looked back at him and prepared for my "Lion King" circle-of-life moment.

"Believe it or not Owen, everyone has something."

He rubbed his eyes and stayed staring at his hands.

"I know you feel like you are the only kid that has to go through this, but you're not alone. Everyone has something. When I was a kid, my mom died and I thought I was the only one to suffer heartbreak, but as I got older I saw that heartbreak comes to everyone in different ways."

He looked at me in the serious introspective way I had came to count on. Then he asked, "What about Marky?" Marky was his older cousin, who he greatly admired.

"Marky?" I asked, not really sure of question.

"Yeah, what does he have?"

"Oh," I said, understanding his train of thought.

"Well . . . Marky, his dad drives a truck and is gone for

long periods of time. He doesn't always get to see his dad all the time either." Owen nodded slightly.

"What about Mitch?" Mitch was a neighbor kid who lived across the street.

"Gosh, Mitch has his baby sister who has special needs, and that can't be so easy all that time"

"How about Kelly and Jill?" A pair of twins in his class.

"Their dad has an addiction where he can't stop drinking, and that causes lots of problems."

I began to wonder how many names he would need to go through, and I was not really sure if dismantling the fantasy of the picket fence was a good idea. But it seemed to be helping. I ran through a few more heart-breaking scenarios.

"Some people go through deaths of a loved one, or having to live in a wheelchair, or not having the money to feed their kids."

I watched him look out at all the people crossing the street, all of them carrying something, some stone of heartbreak, some weight of worry.

Before he got too morose, I pulled him back into the conversation.

"But Owen—these are the things that show us how strong we really are. These are the things that make us into warriors. Do you know that's what your name means?" He looked at me and shook his head.

"Owen means 'young warrior.'"

And then, somehow, Phil's words flew back to me at just the right moment.

"So we get to decide: will we be devastated by these things or will we be devastatingly strong."

I could tell I was on the brink of over selling this idea, and it took every ounce of strength that I had to just hold my tongue and extend instead my feeble faith, a thin and well-worn patchwork blanket that had barely kept me warm at night. He studied my face as I tried to look convincing.

Then he looked back out the window. I couldn't tell if I had been completely successful in extinguishing his doubts, and I was not sure I could live with the discomfort of his sadness. So I turned to my "get out of jail card", every sad single mom's trusted friend: the golden arches.

"Hey!" I said in my most jubilant of Disney princess voices. "Do you want to go get a happy meal?" He looked back to me with a faint smile and a slight nod. Whatever it would take, whatever card I needed to play, I was not above any of it when it came to helping him climb from the chasm of confusion that our separation had tossed him into.

"Okay, let's do it." I pulled my car onto Wilshire and into the flow of life. Two warriors on a quest for happiness, and together we would slay this paper dragon. But first, we would fuel up at the drive-through.

On we went, navigating the rough road of separation and separate households, and sad sons who missed their dads. It did not come with a map. Instead, it held sudden drops and wicked twists, frustrating cul-de-sacs, and disappointing u-turns. The landscape was unpaved and unpleasant.

That night I told Skye about our conversation. She stared back at me thoughtfully.

"We need to plant sunflowers."

"Sorry?"

"All this sadness is toxic, we need to plant some sunflowers. I read that in Hiroshima, after the nuclear disaster, they planted sunflowers to help clean up the environment. Plus, you know sunflowers, they come up in prayer." She pressed her hands together at her chest and bowed to me like a geisha.

"Their little leaves press together, breaking through the soil. And then once they hit the light they spread their leaves and seek the light. We need sunflowers," she confirmed as if it made all the sense in the world. I bowed back to her, not really sure if the solution was sound, but I liked the symbolism of it all. A little more beauty and light couldn't hurt.

By the time I picked Owen up from school she had a dozen packets of seeds and shovels and watering cans. She pulled Owen to the porch and explained that he had a job to do. "You know Jack and the beanstalk?"

"Yeah." Owen smirked and squinted up at her.

"Well get digging, 'cause we got something even better."

"Really?"

She opened her hand and held out a palm of seeds. "These beans are magical, like you and me."

"They look like sunflower seeds," he stated unconvinced.

"Well, yeah because they are seeds, but they are magical like you and me."

"Why."

"Because they have greatness within them." She knelt down as he stared at the little seed.

"How can you tell?" he asked, like a little skeptic. Skye looked up at Owen and gave her notorious smirk back to him.

"I know they just look like stupid little seeds, right? It's easy to get fooled." He stared back at her, not sure if he was supposed to agree. "Everything starts out like a seed. It only grows if you believe in it. So it's best to believe the best about things." Skye held her palm open again, and ran her finger over the seeds. Then with a clear and authoritative voice, she began to tap each one saying, "You have greatness within you and you have greatness within you and you . . . " And on she went until Owen joined in and each seed had been blessed and reminded of its potential. "You have greatness in you," they repeated together.

They smiled at their impromptu ceremony, staring down at the seeds. Skye looked up at him again and said, "C'mon, let's push them into the dirt." He laughed and knelt beside her, and they pressed each seed to the earth as I watched from the stoop— grateful for the seeds and the soil and the Skye and the son.

─ TOOL ─

We will all be pressed to the soil, buried in darkness in one way or another. It can feel like a death, but of course, it is really just our chrysalis. No worthy life escapes a little tenderization, and the getting knocked down is not as interesting as the getting back up. What does not kill us qualifies us for the big work that we are called to do. God does not call the qualified, but qualifies the called. So don't be afraid of your classrooms. Your crucifixions are your catalyst.

The optimal idea is that your life would be a never-ending harmony of affirmations with your Divine. Learning to use your words to speak your truth and affirm the truth of others is how you can transform a hell into a heaven.

It all comes down to your thoughts and words and how you use them. It is done unto you as you believe. If you believe that you are able and capable, the Universe will deliver the resources and support that you need to hurdle any situation.

Your circumstances of today were authored by your thoughts of yesterday. You have the power to perpetuate the celebration or the condemnation. You are co-creating with the Divine and it loves you enough to say "yes." Just like the good dirt says yes to the sprouting seeds. It will nurture even your most brilliant inspirations or your greatest nightmare. Only fear can prevent your manifestation. You are responsible to clear your consciousness of old blocks and ideas. This is not meant to inhibit you, but to empower you. There is no need to tolerate pain and punishment. It serves no one to walk on eggshells, waiting for the other shoe to drop. You have what it takes to break this habit, clear this confusion, and smash this glass ceiling.

⌒ DO THIS ⌒

Learn to affirm yourself and others. An affirmation is a statement that is personal, positive, and present tense. There is a sacred power in the Universe, an energetic resource that is for you, and you can direct it by the power of your word. Through the right use of your word, life can take on a holy and happy glow. You can demonstrate through the power of your word and the passion of your faith.

You don't need to specifically outline your desires. You can trust that God knows you. However, it's good to turn your attention to channeling loving thoughts and words about yourself and others. Say these short affirmations as often as you need reminding. There is no limit to your potential.

Here are a few examples.

I am good, beautiful, and holy.
I have greatness with me.
There is a light within me that cannot fail.
Everything is for me. Nothing is against me.
All is well.

Chapter 5

You Are Entitled

You do not ask too much of life, but far too little.
—A Course in Miracles

I did my best to take it all one day at a time. I stuck to the simple plan, showing up, paying attention, and telling the truth. Simple did not mean easy. There was one commercial shoot where the director was a bit of a creep. It was a four-day shoot in Kansas. On day one, he hit on me, and I turned him down. Aside from being old and odd, he was married. And of course there was my vow of celibacy, which I did not mention because it was not a factor in my decision. He looked at me a bit shocked that I was not interested in hooking up with him.

"Well I am sure you have been hit on by worse, and I have been turned down by better," he commented.

His insinuation made me want to throw up a little. Especially since it seemed to roll off his tongue in such a rehearsed way. How many times had he used that line to lacerate some unwilling actress? On day three of the shoot, the wardrobe lady came to me with a sheer skin-tone bathing suit. She held it up, and I could see right through it like it was made of stocking material, which it was. "This is your costume for the day," she said.

"What?"

"Apparently you have a shower scene." This was not in the script that I had auditioned for. The director had the crew working through the night to build this new set with a shower. I stood there in the wardrobe trailer staring at this body stocking. I was supposed to strip down to nothing, get in this stocking suit, and basically shower in front of everyone? I was mortified and had no idea what to do or say or who to talk to. I had a friend, Eddie, who was working with the crew, and I stood outside the set, smoking one of his cigarettes and trying to settle my nerves.

"It will be over before you know it," he offered. I nodded my head and blew smoke and prayers to the heavens. I am not sure how long it took to shoot the scene. It felt like it went on forever. I was freezing and humiliated and, thank God, they used none of the footage in the actual commercial. I hazard to guess that it was all a power play. By day four, the director was sleeping with one of the extras. As it turns out, he was only half right. He may have been turned down by better, but I had never been hit on by worse. He took the cake.

As the sunflowers began poking through the soil I started to experience a flurry of work, and something interesting happened that I did not expect. Plot twist! Reed began showing up in a different way. It was odd and unsettling at first. I was not sure what to make of it. He started asking me questions and striking up conversations and calling to see how I was doing. "I'm doing fine, I guess," I would answer with trepidation.

The honest answer was, as it turns out, I was doing better than fine. My life was taking a magical turn where I began to take ownership of my happiness. I was making great money doing my art. Owen had made some cool friends, and I was no longer waking in the middle of the night weighted down with fears. Plus, I was becoming physically stronger than I had ever been thanks to all that yoga. And my laughter had returned and was coming easy and often.

Sure, I knew from experience that all this could change, but for the first time in my life, my happiness was based on a foundation that I had built on my own. I was not living on borrowed money, muscle, or faith. This was my house, and I was the righteous ruler, the modest mogul of this humble kingdom. To answer honestly, I was doing great.

Little by little, Reed began sharing with me that he had had an awakening. He even cited the Bible, which was crazy because during our entire relationship he would chastise me for my dumb and limiting religious beliefs.

"How can you believe in a God that does not love everyone equally? Your religion would keep my mom out of heaven because she doesn't believe in Jesus. How is that okay with you?" He asked me these questions as if I had personally made up the rules and was standing at the pearly gates, laughing at his mom in spiritual superiority.

This was the type of argument that he would engage me in on those late lonely nights in Sunnyside, Queens. Having my spiritual roots shaken in such a violent way was debilitating and exhausting. I had never questioned my religious beliefs, that was part of the deal with being Catholic. Don't question. So there again, I hated him for showing me the things I was not willing to look at.

His logical questions made me feel threatened and hoodwinked. How could I be so stupid to believe in such a limited God? I felt pulled by wanting to hold onto my loyalties and wanting to agree with his logic. No matter which side of the fence I landed on, I lost. We went hours with the argument till the landscape of my mind was tilled to the point of trauma. I was a new mom, with a new baby, in a new relationship. I didn't want to go that deep.

"Just let me be, in my unquestioned ignorance," I wanted to say. But that was not an option. Everything needed to be turned over and questioned and all wars needed to be won or no one slept. It was the type of torture they use on prisoners of war. And it worked. I surrendered all that I was to all that he wanted me to be. I tucked in my past and painted over my passion and dumbed down my devotion to deities until all mystic mystery was sedated or solved.

So to have him return to me touting a bible and a belief in spiritual intercession was the most unexpected twist of all. He had just dropped Owen off, and he asked me if I could join him in his car to talk about a few things. I sent Owen to play in the side yard, and I got into the passenger seat.

"It says that a man will leave his father and be united to his wife and the two will become one and that what God joins together, nothing can separate."

It took me a few minutes to recognize that he was not being sarcastic.

"When did you start reading the Bible?" I asked with wide eyes and a true concern for his sanity.

"Well that's the thing, I didn't read it. I just started realizing that I missed my family, and so I pulled out the Bible and just opened it randomly and that was the part my finger fell on! It's incredible, Maureen, and I think what it's saying is that we should get back together."

Here it was, just when I thought it could not get weirder, life played a joker and the whole house of cards began to teeter. How could this be happening? Just when I had finally accepted my situation and realized that I needed to let go, just when I began to get my groove on, just when I had begun to enjoy the taste of freedom, he brought me this.

My atheist "wasband" had come to a spiritual awakening and realized that he missed his old life and flat wife, and he wanted back in. Now the ball was in my court, and instead of serving it back with a big fat YES, I found myself strangely still with a mind of wonders swirling round my brain.

I wanted to trust him and take him back, I wanted to make him happy and be his wife. I wanted to be a "good' Catholic and not be excommunicated from the church. I wanted our old life back too . . . in a way. But I had also tasted life without him. The life that he had warned would crush and kill me turned out to be the life that would qualify and catapult me. I was now semi-soaring in a life that was custom made from my own guidance and gumption. And, truth be told, I loved this new version of me.

Here I was again, torn between two lovers. Do I close up shop and step back in line with his hopes and desires? A guilt that I had not been prepared for settled on. The codependent people-pleaser was woken and willing. But there was also a part of me that knew better. That tool of waiting and checking in with myself was more important now than ever.

"Okay," I said, "well, let me think about that."

My response threw us both off.

"What's to think about? I want to get back together. I want my family back. I am sorry. This was all a big mistake. I am willing to do what it takes to make this work."

Then I somehow remembered my vow to myself. That alone was a real miracle. It may have been the first time that Reed said jump, and I said wait.

"See, the thing is I am not dating anyone for a year. I kind of made this promise to myself."

"Really," he replied like I had just told him I was running for president. "Okay, but we wouldn't actually be dating. We're still officially married," he noted. He definitely should have been an attorney.

"I guess," I agreed. "But also you still officially have that girlfriend," I offered in a morbidly curious attempt to dig for dirt.

"No, she is gone. We are done," he replied, waving his hand as if he was shooing an invisible cat.

"Really?"

"Yeah, I want my life back, my real life."

"Okay, so you would be willing to let her know that?"

"Yeah, yes, of course. It's done, Maureen."

"In front of me."

"What?" He looked at me, his wheels spinning.

"I mean, if it is really done, then you would have no problem saying that in front of her and me." He shifted his weight and stared at the windshield.

"Maureen, it's not like that. It's over. You have to take my word for it."

In the silence I heard myself say, "I don't have to do anything. Your words are empty and mean nothing to me, and if you can't show me that you are sincerely done, then I have no reason to trust or believe you. I am not taking this year off to get back with you. I am taking it off to get back with me." These were some of the hardest words I would ever be asked to speak. I felt guilty that I was not able to be one of those wives that were okay with loose agreements and open relationships. But that was just not my truth, and it was high time that I began honoring my truth.

I got out of the car, shut the door, and stepped up the cement stair with my mother's name in it. From the vantage point of the back stair I watched him pull away, his tires blowing up lose gravel. I could feel his anger and frustration. As hard as it was to be dumped, it was only a million times harder to be the one responsible for not wanting to get our family back together. But this was a pain that I was willing to live with.

What did I want? What did I need? And was I really willing to ask for it? This line of questioning was inspired by watching the way men in my life navigated getting their needs met. Negotiation came after grabbing, demanding, and taking. There was this holy state of entitlement that I wanted to experiment with. A way of navigating decisions with a razor-sharp sword and no apology.

It was not all men, but it was definitely a male characteristic.

There was this one guy that I met at party at the Chateau Marmont, named Carl. The room was abuzz with electricity and B-list actors all looking over each others' shoulders to see who was there and if something better had just walked in the room.

I was standing with Skye and a group of theatre friends and Neve Campbell, who I was trying to place.

"Are you in my acting class?" I asked

She gave me a hard, thoughtful look and shook her head no.

"Well, maybe we met on an audition, because you look so familiar to me."

Skye pushed her eyes out to inform me that I was putting my foot in my mouth.

"Well, I don't really audition anymore," she replied.

"Really?" I asked. "Because you look so familiar, I am sure that we've met. Why aren't you auditioning?"

"Well, I'm on a TV show called *Party of Five*."

"Oh my God, you are!" I laughed. "I am so sorry." Neve excused herself as Skye shot me a look and flitted off to work the room.

On the heels of this brilliance, Carl sauntered over to talk to us.

"So, are you here with anyone?" he asked.

I looked at my girlfriends surrounding us and wondered if they were somehow invisible to him. "You mean a date?" I clarified.

"Yeah." He bobbed his head and looked around the room.

"No, I just got divorced, and I am not dating anyone for a year," I stated. This was more for myself that for him. It was good to remind myself that I was in the midst of an important experiment, an excavation of sorts. Sure, it was dorky, but I had more investment in saving my ass than saving my face.

"Seriously? Divorced?" he said pulling back from me.

His reaction stung. Oh, so this was the type of douchebag that Reed had warned me about. The legend was real.

"Yep," I added with a little bit more confidence than I had expected to deliver.

"Humm," he continued and then replied, "strike one."

I cocked my head and narrowed my eyes at him. "Did you just say, 'strike one?'"

He laughed.

I didn't. I just stared back at him like I was watching a movie. This was the part where the sweaty party predator bares his teeth. I felt myself shrink into my movie seat and cringe at the spot-on bluntness of the author. Except this was not a movie. It was real life.

"So, what do you do?" he asked.

"Well, I do commercials mostly and I run a kids' party company on the weekends, which is great, so I have time to spend with my kid."

Obviously, I had not been groomed in the speed-dating etiquette that happened at Hollywood parties. Apparently, you don't drop the "D" word or the kid situation during the pre-selection ritual.

"You have a kid?" He shot back and shook his body as if he was afraid of catching something. "Strike two!" he announced.

Was this clown kidding me? "And what exactly do you do?"

"Well, I am a writer," he said with an air of elitism. "I've been pitching a few screenplays around town, and they're really picking up some traction."

If I heard this line once, I heard it a million times.

I fought the urge to say, "Strike Three." Instead, I smiled and said, "Oh wow, is that right? Well good for you, buddy." I patted his arm and made my way to the door.

These Hollywood parties were filled with smoke and morons and, being that I was off the market, there was no real reason to subject myself to the appraisal of half-wits.

I bid goodbye to Skye and Bean and grabbed a cab home.

However, the thing that peaked my interest was the audacious way that men could be so down and dirty about what worked for them and what would not. And the permission that they gave themselves to just speak their thoughts and make their request without edits.

"I want my family back."

"I've been shot down by better."

"Strike two!"

It gave me pause to really think about how I might indulge my own game plan with less sentimentalism. I was genuinely happy that I was taking this sex sabbatical so that I could adequately stand back and watch the way things work. I began looking at relationships the way a director would look at characters in a play. I began seeing the scaffolding that was to blame for the shit show of modern day relationships.

Oh, look there is this power struggle. Oh wow, did you see that self-betrayal? Oh no, this is the part where she caves. I was starting to see a pattern, a recipe that had been passed down from one generation to the next.

Boy meets girl and falls in love with her flight. Girl falls in love with his anchor. Boy tucks girl under his wing to keep her safe. In doing so, he crushes her wings. But this is forgivable, because he offers protection, power, and prosperity. Girl is encouraged to step into the cage of conformity. She hands over her name at the door. Girl settles in to being a captured and caged beauty. Society keeps her distracted with consumerism and setting up nests and the unrelenting assessments of her abilities, looks, and logic. She sees all the ways that she falls short and begins to feel stuck and vulnerable. Boy looks in the cage but does not recognize the cage's creature. Boy gets distracted by a new fancy in flight. Boy leaves girl. And scene.

I began to witness how women were systematically encouraged to surrender to these scripts and structures, then raised on scarcity, and finally groomed for supplication. Play nice, don't expect much,.and don't ask for more.

The roles that I was auditioning for were limited to the

happy shiny mom or happy sexy girlfriend. This lopsided fairy-tale was woven into our social tapestry and tribal agreements.

None of the Disney princesses had mothers, but they sure as hell all had a hero. Every audition I went on I would see little girl actresses being primped and groomed by their mothers like lap dogs while the little boys got to run the halls screaming and laughing. I felt the injustice in my bones, it got under my skin and made me itchy and bitter.

"Get married to a man who can take care of you," was a subtle and yet searing way to say, "You won't be able to take care of yourself." Then, while you're at it, give up your job, give up your power, and oh, just for good measure, if this system does not do the job of getting you to forget yourself, give up your name. Give up your name! This would be a huge classroom for me. A big undoing that was caustic and costly and painful. If you get anything from this book, I hope you get this: do not surrender your name to a man, no matter what. This is an archaic entrapment that needs to be put to rest.

You are entitled to hold onto your identity, and if having a unified family name matters, then simply request that he take yours. At least let it be a conversation that you have together. Just because it has always been a certain way does not make it optimal. This is not as big a hurdle as you would imagine. Gay and lesbian relationships have been figuring it out.

Stripping you of your name is like removing from you the ability to leave your own mark on the world. It removes your authorship, responsibility, and visibility, leaving a legacy of children sent out into the word with the branding of only the father. This is just one area where we have tended to just go along without stopping to question if it is still working for us. Why is it just assumed? Why are we still accepting a patriarchy that encourages us to be delivered and branded like property from one man to another? If we don't contemplate all of our choices, we will not have true choice. Being that we are products of our choices, we need to get more intimate with what those choices are.

I began to see how unconscious I was around so many things. I saw how I was part of the problem, how I had given up my power and willingly fell into the myth of damsel in distress. There was a universally approved annihilation of the feminine power that was perverse and pervasive. It would take a clear-headed woman not to lose herself in the confining roles that society had drafted for her demise.

The way to maintain this hierarchy of power is to continue to infuse the communal conversation with the fear of death, danger, and dragons that are insurmountable. As Reed had been groomed to warn me, "It's tough out there in the real world, and no one will want you."

This is the type of script that causes good women to fold.

There I was, carrying the warped message to the new crop of impressionable girls with my parties. With every wave of my wand, every bat of my lashes, I was teaching the techniques of magical thinking when I should have been teaching empowerment. I began to change my tune.

It's no mistake that most Disney Princesses have dead or absent mothers. If a mother is present, then she is represented by the archetype of a wicked stepmother. From Belle, to Pocahontas, to Snow White, Ariel, and Cinderella. Where had all the mothers gone?

We've been marinating in these stories of disempowerment. They have killed our mothers and turned our crones to witches and bitches. Then, just for good measure, shower the maidens with anti-aging campaign. There is no hope for happiness in this select script. Sure, we all have stories and ways of seeing things and ways that we want others to see us, but if the story does not line up with the truth, we are not doing anybody any favors.

We project these ideas out onto the world and unconsciously hide our fears in those around us, judging them for the things we don't have tolerance or compassion for. These broken-down stories prevent us from true connection. I found I was longing for true connection, transparency, integrity, and honesty.

I became even more committed to getting down to the bones and stripping away the fantasy. I longed for real conversation and had no time or tolerance for bullshit. I craved the autumns of New Jersey and how nature stripped down to nothing and let it all fall away. Just let it all go. That is how I felt, and I was kind of okay with it, visible and vacant and yet oddly vital. I was gaining a new attraction and appreciation for the ability to shed the mask and move in reality. I wanted real even if real was raw.

I began to remember and reclaim a kinder idea about myself. I whispered affirmations, "I am capable. I got this. Everything is for me." I was ready to lay down the illusion of victim and step into warrior.

I remembered when my mother lost all her hair to cancer and decided to be a baby for Halloween. She sported an adult diaper, a onesie, a rattle, and a smile. Her baby-bald head held high with no apologies and no desire for sympathy. Her only goal was fun. There was a power in that. To witness a woman shed the confines and show up with her warts and wrinkles and riddles and lay all her cards out. I wanted that kind of fearlessness.

I was taking this time to do exactly that. To stand in the stillness even after the hair was cut off, the marriage had dissolved into murky water, and the sunflowers were only silent concepts lurking in the seeds. I needed to wash it all away and begin anew. I needed to reclaim my name.

It became important to me. I was born the sixth daughter, which has none of the mystical privileges reserved for the seventh son. By the time I arrived, my parents had used their favorite girl name as well as their second favorite girl name not to mention their third, fourth, and fifth. Still, I didn't do too badly. I was christened Maureen Rose Pierson, and it was with this fine moniker that I would begin my life and later my career as an actress.

I remember, at the start of my career, I was pretty clueless. My dad had a friend named Mr. Larkin who was a TV actor, but he went by Mickey Muldoon. I went to talk to him about being an actor, and he told me everything he knew. "How do you get an agent? Where do you get pictures? How do you book a job?" I was a thirsty little sponge, and he was a generous wellspring of wisdom. It was his final answer that I should have paid greater attention to. "Why the stage name?" I asked.

"People will remember Mickey Muldoon more than Jim Larkin, and your job is to get folks to remember you." I nodded, closed my notebook, and trudged off in the direction of my dreams.

During my marriage to Reed, I decided not to take on his last name for my career because it was basically a tongue twister. It was the type of name that no one could pronounce, and no one would remember. But I did take it on for general use sometimes like making dinner reservations, or for a library card.

Now with the impending divorce, it was time for me to make a name change, and this time for good. Reed's last name was not one that I had a problem shedding. But I did have a problem. I was in name limbo. I couldn't see keeping my married name, but it also didn't feel right returning to my maiden name. I was not sure I'd ever get married again. However, I was sure I would never again change my name. I wanted to pick my own name and stick with it. I wanted a name that would suit me for life. I looked over my family names. My mother's maiden name was Rustia, and that did not feel like a match. Then I looked at my grandmother's name, which as fate would have it was actually Muldoon, like Mickey. So, Maureen Muldoon it was.

I re-christened myself Maureen Rose Muldoon and headed back to work with a greater sense of self. I was Maureen Muldoon of the Jersey Muldoons. It was a name that just felt right. It also turned out to be a stroke of genius.

People loved saying the name. "Maureen Muldoon," they would call out with an Irish lilt when I went in for auditions.

"Maureen Muldoon," they would repeat as they took me in. This new name literally made them smile in a way I had not noticed before. My fair skin, freckles, and red hair caused them to smirk across the desk at me as if they had discovered a leprechaun. This never happened when I was Maureen Pierson and never ever when I was using Reed's name. I can't say Maureen Muldoon was a better actress, but she sure booked more jobs and made a more lasting impression than either of the other Maureens. Was Mickey Muldoon right all along? Was it really just the name? To me, it felt like everything.

Now that I was reclaiming myself and renaming myself I began asking, "What did I want?"

What I really wanted was to spend time with my sisters. So, I called them up and invited them for a long weekend. There is nothing like sister medicine, and when they arrived, I realized how much I missed them. Skye was right again, there is something so restorative and healing about connecting with your roots.

— TOOL —

You are entitled to miracles, you are a beloved daughter of the Divine. It's time to stop underestimating yourself. It's time to name and ask for what you want. *A Course in Miracles* says that we don't ask too much, we ask far too little. Most of us have not been taught how to ask for more. We've been told that it's greedy or bad to ask. So we have to bust through some old programing and get our entitlement on. Acknowledging, asking, and accepting MORE is a game changer.

— DO THIS —

Look at all the titles that you carry: Sister, daughter, mother, employee, boss, voter, traveler, homeowner, and driver are just a few possibilities. Each of these titles comes with responsibility and privleges. Empowerment comes when we stop allowing ourselves to be enabled, when we stop allowing the status quo, and when we stop living unexamined lives. Trust yourself. You know how to steer your own life. You are the authority when it comes to you.

Stop ordering off the menu, ask for what you want, and know all your choices.

Focus on where your life is working and where you feel fully lit. Take the time to notice the feelings that you have when immersed in these positive experiences.

Then when you find yourself in one of these optimal experiences, look around, take in the moment, and then say, "Thank you, more please." So often we give God a to-do list of wants and desires and we forget to really notice and appreciate when things are unfolding in our favor. Asking for more from a place of gratitude will open doors for many blessings.

Do not worry. Worry is planning for something that you do not want. Plan for things to work out in your favor.

As you rewire your mind and allow yourself to feel and celebrate your good fortune, and as you continue to take small thoughtful steps towards your optimal outcome, your good will begin to take form. With persistence, your actions and affirmations will build and birth a greater good than you even knew to ask for. So ask bigger, and ask for more. The Divine is in the business of extravagant serendipities and She will roll out the red carpet Herself for you.

Chapter 6

Invest In Yourself

Be happy for your only function here is happiness.
—*A Course in Miracles*

Having my sisters come for a visit was nothing short of a blood transfusion. They were the vital water to my dying houseplant. Not to be too dramatic, but it's not until you're around people who really know you that you can tell how far off course you have gone.

The visit was filled with wine and laughter, and of course an impromptu fashion show in my backyard where they decided it would be fun to try on all of the Disney Princess costumes and do a photoshoot.

It was a long weekend that felt way too short. They ended their stay with a visit to the theater company with me for our Monday night workshop. While we were there, I got on stage and shared another song from my brokenhearted repertoire. It was something about being sideswiped and flattened, something about being cut loose in the deep end, and learning how to swim. Again, totally cringe-worthy.

I could see Skye making her bad blue cheese face at me again. I stood in the limelight preparing for the feedback from the other artists. This was always an interesting experience, because people could say whatever they wanted to the performer and the performer was to respond with two words, "Thank you." The group was a mix of young and old, green and seasoned, artists and writers of all flavors and styles. Sometimes the comment section was the most entertaining part. The group could be counted on for an interesting batch of opinions.

There was this one guy named Will, who happened to be there that night. He raised his hand to share his thoughts. I nodded to him.

"What I love about your work is that it's very transparent. Brave, you know? You just put it all out there in a very generous way, and I can tell that it's not manufactured emotions. It's real, and I think it's great."

I sat back down between my sister, and they both started elbowing me in the ribs.

"Who is that guy?"

"Yeah, who is Mr. Comments?"

I nudged them back. "Stop, he's like engaged or something."

"Maureen, you're crazy. He is all about you."

They spent the rest of the class making eyes at each other and swooning every time Will added his voice to the conversation.

I didn't think much of it, but of course my sisters grabbed that ball and ran with it for miles.

"Oh my God, Maureen! Did you see the way that he looked at you? Did you see the way that he made those long comments about you? He didn't say anything like that to anyone else, but he couldn't stop talking about you." They started referring to him as "Mr. Comments." That would become his nickname.

For the rest of the night, until they got on the plane, they went on and on about how I should hook up with Mr. Comments. I told them what I told everyone in earshot that year.

"I am not hooking up with Mr. Comments or anyone for twelve months."

This was a promise I had made to myself, and although I had deserted myself a million ways prior to this one commitment, I was somehow sticking with it.

Plus, there was the fact that Mr. Comments was also dealing with a visitation from cancer. Will was a model who had traveled the world, spoke three different languages, and graduated from Brown. He was a great actor and writer, and at twenty-six years old, he also had stage III Hodgkin Lymphoma. Although he seemed to be getting better, the guy had cancer. This just might not be a great time to engage in a relationship for him either.

I did not really know him outside of theater group. He mostly kept to himself, but I did notice that he was going through a bit of a change too. It wasn't just his hair and body that the cancer had taken down a notch, it was his spirit. Where once there stood a cocky post-collegiate young man, was now a guy mid-fight and well tenderized by life.

Cancer had been putting him through the wringer. His golden-boy looks had been ravaged. He was bald, bloated, and beaten. When he said I was brave, I thought, *Look who's talking.* Cancer was not an easy classroom for anyone to navigate, but doing it at twenty-six against the backdrop of the bold and the beautiful of Los Angeles—that was brave.

Honestly, there was a place within me that was intrigued by my sisters' assessment of the situation, and specifically, Mr. Comments.

You see, when I first met Mr. Comments, I was dumbstruck. My heart skipped. I felt complete imbalance. The guy was gorgeous, like the make-you-stop-in-your-tracks-and-lose-your-train-of-thought kind of gorgeous.

I was sitting in the theater the first day he arrived, and I am pretty sure I gasped. It was the feeling that you get when you rush to the train station and run up the stairs to the platform only to witness your train pull away. Then you stand there as all the ramifications of that missed train begin to dawn on you. And slowly, the rush of adrenaline fades and all you are left with is the sweaty shock of your own horrible, unfortunate bad timing.

When I first saw Will, I was married to Miss Universe's boyfriend, but married nonetheless. After seeing him, my first thought was, *Oh my God, he is so gorgeous.* My second thoughts was, *Oh my God, I am so married.*

This line of thinking was totally unsettling and strange. I was not the type of woman to check out other men. Especially because I was married to a very jealous and controlling man who accused me of looking at men even when I wasn't, so I was super vigilant to not linger on anyone. That part of me had been effectively shut down. Except that day when Will walked in, then it wasn't.

As startling as my first two thoughts were, my third thought was even odder. I had this real and visceral feeling that ushered in the feeling that I had somehow married the wrong person. Like I had taken a wrong turn somewhere or I had experienced a wrinkle in time. It was completely disconcerting, and it took me a little while to shake it from my bones. I convinced myself that it was insane. Will was a presence. I am sure he made many women feel like they had married the wrong guy!

I shrugged it off, piled my tipsy sisters on to a plane, and waved good-bye. After they left, things really started picking up. I was booking more parties than I could handle and started subbing work out to other unemployed actors. Basically, I was a party pimp for Disney princesses. You want a Belle, an Ariel, a Cinderella. I got you covered. I was hired by the wife of a prominent TV star to do magic and face painting at their Bel Air home. It was a western party, and they didn't want a character, just someone to show up with a cowboy hat and boots to talk in a drawl and entertain the kids.

When I got to the backyard, where the party was taking place, there was Carl—the writer from the Chateau Marmont—with a baby cowboy hat on his head working the bar. It crushed and delighted me. What were the chances of a big-time writer working the bar? I don't mean to sound bitter, but the guy had given me a strike for having a kid!

LA had a twisted way of turning her cheek on you. It could be an erratic pendulum. You never knew when karma would bite you in the ass. One day, you're serving drinks at the Four Seasons, and the next day, you are throwing a party there. Things happened fast. It was smart to not be a dick on either end of the seesaw.

I made my way to the bar to order a Coke and cut through the awkwardness. He made a B-line to my B cup, which was as much an illusion as his writing career.

Amid all these changes and ups and downs, that was the only constant. That was the shadow that followed me into every exchange and encounter. I was still completely and totally obsessed with breasts, with *my* breasts, or lack of breasts. Like stupidly obsessed.

Breasts peered down at me from every billboard and waved from the advertisements on busses. They sat next to me at every audition and pressed against me in every friend's hug. There was no avoiding them. I thought about plastic surgery. I read all the fine print on chest enhancement pills. I did all the exercises to lift the ladies, and I continued to keep the Wonderbra corporation in business. I was plagued with that feeling of inadequacy. I knew that it was the least important thing about me, but it felt like the most important thing. The bulletproof bras that I was wearing made me feel like a fraud, and it was hard to imagine getting intimate with someone for fear that they would see my shortcomings.

At one party in Malibu, I met a woman named Liberty. She was a long-legged beauty with an incredible afro. We were working a kids' circus party together at this palatial home over-looking the water. It was owned by a Hollywood attorney who was dressed as a ringmaster and his wife who was a bearded woman. I am pretty sure there was an inside joke under the cos-tumes that was begging to come out. Their daughter Huan, who they adopted from China was thrilled to be celebrating her fifth birthday. She whipped around the party wearing a *Lion King*-type headdress and peddling a shiny unicycle while managing to spin a baton and scream nonsensical words at anyone and everyone. Huan was a refreshing change from the usual drill of princess pink and plastic tiaras.

I was there as a clown who could do magic, and Liberty was hired to juggle and do gymnastics while dressing in a sparkly bodysuit. She sidled up and started stretching out her limbs.

"Girl, check this crib, huh?"

"Seriously you could get lost going to the bathroom."

"No kidding." She moved her body gently, leaning and stretching and then letting out a low moan.

"I have no idea how this is gonna go down." She patted her breast and whispered in at me. "The girls are new."

"Oh wow!" I replied now unable to take my eyes from her breasts.

"Yep, you know I tried the whole estrogen route, but they just never took off, so I ordered myself a double latte. I cannot believe I waited this long to get them. Best decision ever, well after coming out as trans."

"Oh, really?" I said.

"You couldn't tell?" She asked.

"No. I. No!" Liberty was like a black Angelina Jolie, and I would have never guessed that she was transgender.

"I hope the girls stay put, I gotta fling and flip my ass all over the yard, and the last thing I need is to have my Brad Tits blow up at a kid's party." She laughed and adjusted her studded bodysuit. Then she turned her chest to me.

"Do they look okay?" She asked with complete sincerity.

She was a foot taller, and so I stood eye level with the most beautiful breasts in the world. My red clown nose was almost pressed into her cleavage.

"They are perfection," I whispered and traveled back up her neck to her smooth chin and her million-dollar smile. It was surely one of the happiest smiles I had seen in a while. I tried to imagine her as a boy, but I couldn't see it.

"Was it painful?" I asked.

She nodded, closed her eyes, and rubbed her pursed lips together.

"Oh Girl, like I say, Liberty ain't free." She opened her eyes and smiled down at me. "Beauty comes at a cost, baby. But it was worth it."

Soon the music started, and Liberty flung herself around the yard like a human explosive. Flying and rolling, high kicks and splits, and then she ended her dance by juggling the fire sticks. It was a hard act to follow.

It was not just her talent and flexibility; it was her unedited command and confidence. The kids stared in awe. And when she was done, they ran to her and begged for more. She rolled out a mat and instructed the kids on how to tuck and roll and jump. She taught them how to shake and shimmy, and I am sure no one but the Ringmaster, who seemed to have a special attraction to Liberty, was any the wiser. Liberty and Huan hit it off and I marveled at the way amazing way the Universe has at bringing people together. I wanted what they were having, not so much the breasts, or the beauty, but the unedited happiness.

It was odd to have such an obsession with breasts, because for a long time I wanted nothing to do with them. After witnessing my mother's battle with breast cancer, they actually scared the hell out of me. I was ten when her cancer arrived, and if that was what happened to people with breasts, I wanted nothing to do with them.

I willed myself to not to grow breasts. And I didn't. I can't say for sure that it was mental, but I know it was not genetics. All my sisters had pretty large breasts, one of them a double D, capital letters, and yet in keeping with my prayer, I had been successful in growing none at all. At the time, I didn't care! The breasts on other girls just seemed like unnecessary baggage that would one day kill you.

Breasts were to blame for this whole experience. Breasts had ushered Reed in to my life, and breasts had ushered him out. Breasts were obviously the problem and not worth all the trouble, and yet I still really wanted them.

There I was, this flat-chested single mom who had been dumped for Miss Universe and her perfect breasts. I kept thinking that if I still had my beautiful pregnancy breasts, I would still be married. And for some reason, I cannot explain why, I began mourning my mom. I grieved her, her breasts, my breasts, my husband, I mourned for the woman I wasn't. Fully mourning my mother would mean accepting that she was gone. Honoring these feelings helped me to heal the place in me that had felt deserted. I began to see a pattern of how I had believed I was abandonable. Reed was only playing the part that I had unconsciously held out to him. My script said I am abandonable. Reed apparently had a script that read, I will abandon people. We were a match made in hell.

I was finally getting down to the core belief. I wrote the words, "I am not abandonable" on a note card and stuck it to the mirror in our little bathroom. Skye answered back with a post of her own that said, "never."

What happened next was hard to explain. I took those chicken cutlets and tossed them in the trash, the padding, the underwires, and all bulletproof bras. Out they went.

Then I decided I wanted the real deal. I wanted breasts and

I was no longer afraid to actually have them. I called a plastic surgeon, made an appointment and I went out and got myself the real deal. Or rather the fake deal . . . either way they were mine. A beautiful pair of breasts.

This was no small thing. I went under the knife, which I said I never would. I spent a load of cash, which I did not really have. When it was all said and done, I knew what Liberty felt like.

It was not Barbie-Doll boobs I was after, just enough to fill out a bra and relieve me of my obsession. And that is exactly what I got. I know I may have gotten caught in the booby trap. But they make me happy, and we all deserve to be happy. Go ahead and flip to the cover and check out my fake boobs. I'll wait here.

Nice, right?

But the first day I had serious buyer's remorse. It was horrific. I was vomiting and in pain and regretting the decision with every thread of my being. It was a twenty-four-hour nightmare.

The second day, I woke up happier than I had been in years. Like really freakin' happy. All that from a pair of breasts? Why?

A huge believer in healing things from the inside out, I am not the type of person that would promote buying your way out of a problem. So it seemed strange. Plus, there was all the social commentary in my head. The cultural stigma that said doing something like this was trashy and cheap and wrong and cheating. So why did they make me feel so good? Honestly, and I know I am obliged to sing a different song, but to this day they are still two of the nicest things I have ever done for myself. Maybe it was not just about filling out my bra, maybe it was about listening to myself and taking myself seriously and investing in me, even if that seemed selfish and shallow. We are all such beautiful and complex beings.

This is not the right answer for everyone. But if you want to pierce, tattoo, or nip-tuck you own personal meat suit, that is for you and only you to decide.

I don't regret it, not at all. Every once in a while, you just need a happy meal and that's all there is to it.

‿ TOOL ‿

Trust and Invest in Yourself

Showing up, paying attention, and telling the truth about your deepest desires is radical self-care. It's time you invest in yourself without shame. Do not be the last priority on your list. Why be a martyr when you could be amazing? There is nothing more helpful than a happy woman. So, put your money where your truth is.

We become more intimate with our true north when we get real about our own warts, riddles, and wants. Let me give you a tip here, men are not in the business of over analyzing their desires. They give themselves full permission to trust and invest without shame or exception.

‿ DO THIS ‿

Invest in yourself

It could look like many things: buying a new dress, a new camera, a trip that you have been wanting to take. Put the down payment down, let your friends and family know it's happening, and then do it. Life is short, produce the song, rent that office, hire the coach, take the class, or get the boobs. Trust yourself, do not live by the rules and judgments of others, and do not apologize for your happiness. You deserve to be happy.

If you are riding the fence trying to decide on an investment, especially if it is an investment that will move your message forward, take this as a sign that maybe you should go for it.

Chapter 7

Show Up

A teacher of God is anyone who chooses to be one . . .
somewhere he has made a deliberate choice in which
he did not see his interests as apart from someone else's.
—*A Course in Miracles*

That July, I was invited back to New Jersey for my dear friend's wedding. Colleen and I had grown up together, and now it was her turn to tie the knot. The ceremony was at our old church, Our Lady of Sorrows, and I was asked to be one of the bridesmaids. I stared down at the invitation and went through the mental rolodex of all the reasons why I could not or should not attend. It would mean flying home for a long weekend. There was the money and the time and leaving Owen with Reed and my general shame of facing all the questions of, "how is married life?"

Plus, I was not sure I believed in the concept of weddings and marriage and happily ever after any more. Colleen left several messages on my machine when my RSVP card never arrived. In the end, despite my hesitation, I still believed in showing up for my friends. Plus, I hated the idea of missing a good happy hour.

I held a frozen smile as I stood staring down the aisle at her and the insane parade of paternal entitlement on display. Here she was, a hugely successful business woman, holding the arm of her father, who was proudly and ritualistically "giving her away" to another man. Like cattle. It felt like such an antiquated tradition and, despite my trying to play it cool, I felt my blood boil. I looked around at all the other genuinely happy people smiling at the beautiful bride. It was as if I was watching a completely different movie. I could see they were enjoying a romance, and yet I was watching a horror film. A horror film where my best friend was cast as the dumb blonde who goes to check out the sound in the basement. All my internal alarms were going off.

Our mutual friend, Beth, stood beside me. Back in our school days Colleen, Beth, and I were thick as thieves. We had stood on this very altar since we were kids watching the baptisms of our baby brothers and sisters, bowing our heads for our first holy communions, taking on new names for our confirmations, and now here we stood to witness each other's weddings. There was a time that I loved being up here by the altar. There was a time that I thought priests were like rock stars.

Priests got to do all the fun stuff. They waved the incense and doled out the host; they had the super power to absolve sinners. And, on sweltering hot summer days, when you begged for a breeze to finds its way into the chapel, they flicked holy water at you. It looked like a fun gig, but it was more than just my love for the pomp and ritual of the Catholic service that drew me to the altar like a kid to the circus. What I loved the most about priests was that they had the power and the platform, they used it to share stories that could change people's lives forever and for the better.

They celebrated the new babies and new marriages and new members of our community. They sancitfied and celebrated everything good. Could there be a better way to spend our hours? My bold, little heart did not think so.

When we were asked as little kids, I remember hearing all the boys and girls declaring what they wanted to be, firemen and mommies and doctors and bankers. Me? I wanted to be a priest.

We had a couple great priests in our parish, and I looked forward to hearing what they had to say. I didn't understand most of the stuff they read from the Bible, but I loved how they applied it to real life. Sure, every once in a while, you would get a snoozer, but for the most part, they were a nice bunch of quick-witted storytellers who ended every sermon with, *"Go in peace, to love and serve the world."* I was not exactly sure what *"love and serve the world"* meant, but I liked it.

My willingness would only take me so far. I had a major road-block—it was my vagina. I had lady parts and ladies played no part in the service as far as I could see. The only time I ever saw a lady on the altar was when they were there to sing a song.

As I got older, I needed to understand the riddle and reasoning behind it all. These questioned tormented me, and in turn, I would torment the nuns.

"Sister, why can't girls be priests? Why is it just Sunday that we're supposed to keep holy? Why do you have to dress like that?"

The list of questions went on and on. Most of the time, they would just shake their heads and ignore me, and other times they would furrow their brows and scold me.

"Maureen, don't be so bold!" I began to equate asking questions with being bold and being bold with being bad. I didn't get it. I perceived the lack of equality; but, at the same time, my Inner Teacher was whispering that all was perfect. I was confused about why God would give me the desire to be a priest yet place me in a world that made it impossible to fulfill that desire.

I spent both my childhood and adolescence at this church and the school attached to it, being told, "Don't ask so many questions." I wanted to understand and make sense of things, even at the risk of having my questions met with frustration and disapproval. I don't blame the nuns. I'm sure that my curiosity overwhelmed and exhausted them. Yet I couldn't stop myself; I had questions and I wanted answers!

"You can't be a priest, Maureen, but you can be a nun."

"A nun? No offence, sister, but I don't want to be a nun." This was met with an icy stare that informed me that I was an inch away from being smacked with a ruler. So after the endless barrage of scolding from the nuns and snickering from the boys, I began to fold up my dreams and surrender my hopes. A lady priest was a blasphemous sacrilegious claim that could get you tossed into hell, or worse, laughed at.

I stopped asking questions and looked back on the menu for socially and spiritually approved careers for curious girls with big mouths and too many questions. That was when I decided to be an actress.

Here I was, years later; in the place that both raised me up and shut me down, dressed as a bridesmaid watching Colleen make her way down the aisle in the pre-requiste white. A symbol of her purity linked not to her soul but her sex, specifically her sexual status. This vesseled virgin escorted to the altar as a pre-sex ritual. Was I the only one seeing this?

"She looks so happy," Beth whispered.

"Yeah, and sometimes salt looks like sugar," I whispered back.

Beth gave me an evil eye, and I reminded myself to play nice. I looked out at my beautiful friend, her smile shining even beneath the veil. I willed myself to smile back and gave the best performance I could muster under the circumstances. When the holy charade was over, we made our way outside.

I was grateful for the fresh air and found myself taking in deep breaths while we waited in the hot July sun for the church to empty. *What a full-on farce,* I thought as we all turned to witness Colleen trip down the steps, grasping a handful of dress and an armful of husband, smiling with the drunken gaze of one who had been over-served on fairy tales.

My stomach felt tight and my mouth was dry. *How tragic,* I thought, feeling a flash of envy for my friend's blissful ignorance while at the same time fighting the urge to rush through the crowd of unhappily married relatives and rescue her from all the lies that she had just bought into.

This was a small community, and most people knew each other. So most people knew that I was fresh from separation and heading to divorce, if it had not already happened. I felt the eyes of a hundred sorrowful souls penetrating me. I could almost feel the red letter "A" being embroidered into my dress with every sideways glance and every cupped whisper that sent eyes shooting my way. Even though I was not the guilty party, I felt like I was being branded all the same for not being able to make the marriage work.

It was my first neighborhood wedding since Reed moved out, and I was surprised by my emotions. I thought that I had dealt with it, but the whole wedding thing was bringing a lot up. There was anger, sadness, confusion, and a whole slew of other emotions that I had yet to identify names for. I continued to take deep breaths and fight back the tears that threatened to give me away. It was no use; they bubbled up despite my best efforts, salty separation tears spilling from my eyes and splashing down my cheeks.

Of course this was a normal reaction at a wedding, joyous tears for the happy bride. But I knew, and secretly so did everyone else, that these were mourning tears for my own slaughtered marriage.

I could not help thinking of all the women who wept at my wedding. Were those tears for themselves? My neck grew warm wondering about it. It made me wish that I had been warned. I took a deep breath and tried to shake off my cynicism. My face began to throb as I noticed how hard I was trying to smile. I was disgusted with myself, how grossly obvious, how sinfully pathetic. I lowered my head into my purse to search for a non-existing tissue as the newlyweds headed for the limo. I reassured myself that this torture would be over soon. At the reception, I would swallow it all down with a few glasses of vino.

I looked up in time to see the sea of tight faces turning my way, in time to see the flying bouquet zeroing in on me, in time to step back and let it hit the pavement.

A lifetime seemed to pass before the flock of unmarried women tackled the booty like Black Friday shoppers. They grabbed and tugged and wrestled each other, sending up a shower of petal confetti and laughter from the crowd. It sickened me to think that this was a form of entertainment. I stood like a statue, a frozen spectator, assigned to witness the carnage.

"Stop!" I wanted to yell. "It's not worth it! Trust me!"

I was super grateful when Beth's voice penetrated my shock.

"Let's head to the reception, shall we?" She tapped my shoulder several times lightly to wake me from my nightmare.

We climbed into her old car, rolled down the windows, and she made a few attempts before the car kicked into gear. Out in front of us was the statue of the Blessed Mother. I had spent a lot of hours kneeling before her, trying to figure out why my mom had cancer, and what prayers could save her, and how maybe the Blessed Mother could help heal her. Because I believed in those things at that time. And then I didn't, and now here I was again, wondering about the mystery of miracles and healing, and not really convinced that it was ever really possible to begin with.

There was a long line of cars exiting the parking lot, hoping to make a mad dash to the happy hour. As we navigated to the exit, I took in the familiar landscape. Our Lady of Sorrows's parking lot was nothing short of iconic, a steep gravel hill that we kids christened "Sorrow's Hill."

It was just a black gravel top parking lot where people parked on Sundays, and during the school year it was used as a play yard. How they got away with calling it a "play yard" is beyond me. There was nothing playful about it. I looked out over the cracks and potholes and loose rocks and thought about all the unsuccessful games of kick-ball and spud, when the ball would inevitably find its way to the very bottom of the hill. Play never had a chance.

There was the one faded hopscotch board where Lilly Towle had her fated hop-scotch accident, when she peed herself on number seven. After that, everyone lost interest in hopscotch.

I could still hear the echo of Mrs. Powell's voice, the grumpy playground attendant, who did double duty as the crossing guard. She was also the poor slob that got tossed out there on the parking lot with all of us kids and told to keep the peace. That was the type of job you gave to a mom who could not make the tuition but still wanted the Catholic education. That was a position that even the nuns frowned upon.

Mrs. Powell seemed to be married to that parking lot. The first time I saw her was the first time I encountered the parking lot. It swept me off my feet. I was walking to kindergarten with my oldest sister Mary who was in charge of delivering me to my destination. The wind was so strong, and I was small, and when we met up, the wind won. While crossing the street to the kindergarten, it picked me up, my feet moonwalking over the crosswalk, barely touching the ground. Mrs Powell yelled to my sister, "Hold that kid down!"

And then at the corner, a gust of wind whipped up and lifted me straight into the air to where my sister had to grab me by the ankle like I was a human kite. From that height I caught my first real glimpse of the parking lot. It seemed to go on for miles and miles even though it was only a block long.

I learned everything I needed to learn from that parking lot. All the rhythms and riddles and rules of life. All the stories and songs and secrets of childhood.

Miss Mary Mack, all dressed in black.
And a knick and a knack and an old paddy wack
if you stepped on a crack, you could break your mom's back.
You'd carry your lunch in an old paper sack
and if a nun hits you . . . you don't hit her back.

I discovered my resourcefulness on that "playground," while crushing on Patrick Larson, my first love.

Every night, I would write in my diary. *Dear Patrick, I love you. I don't know if you love me back. Ho well, Maureen.* I didn't know that I was writing, *"Ho well."* I thought I was writing "Oh well." I had dyslexia. I figured it out when my sisters found my diary, read it, and began to tease me for the next ten years. "Oh look, it's raining. Ho well!"

There I was, being chased by Patrick Clayton, my love, my dream boy, my everything. He chased after me as he had done for all the days before. I dutifully played my part as prey. Running from his advances. But that day I had a spark of inspiration. *Why am I running from what I want?* I thought. In that moment of enlightenment, I stopped, turned around, threw out my arms, and waited with a smile for him to fall into my embrace. What actually happened was that he saw me, stopped short, screamed like a girl, and went running in the opposite direction. I was completely amused by this response. I could scare a boy! I could be the hunter instead of the hunted.

Then there was that awkward moment one winter day, while freezing my ass off, I had another spark of inspiration. I approached the cool kids to try and convince them to create an igloo out of our coats, so we could huddle together inside. My genius idea was met with the eye roll of Bridget Hall, who informed me, "No, Maureen, we're not doing that!" So, I found my way to a smaller circle of odd ball kids like me, where I learned to swear in Spanish and curse in pig Latin. UckFAY OuYay, erndetBEY. I was never very good at it.

Everything happened on that parking lot. It was the holy ground, where Kelly Turner would perform a wedding ceremony for Jenny Yerman and Robert Conners. Complete with "the kissing of the bride." This unholy and unsanctioned matrimony sent the nuns into a frenzy. Jealous much? As punishment, all the kids had to stay after school, except for me because I was the nerd who had gone home for lunch that day and missed the whole blessed event.

On snow days, Sorrows Hill was the place to be. My sisters would grab our sleighs and inner tubes and garbage can lids and go flying down Sorrows hill. This was where I experienced flight for the second time, when we took a trip down in a shopping cart just for kicks. Upon realizing that we were in imminent danger of crashing, Mary yelled for us to JUMP. Which I did. Arms spread, eyes wide. Feeling like superman. For a brief and rewarding second before my body met with the pavement and I landed like road kill.

This holy haven of Sorrows Hill was the spot that hosted our yearly school carnival, where we kids would ride the Ferris wheel and scream like banshees on the salt and pepper ride as we gripped the bars with sticky cotton candy hands. At my eighth-grade graduation, it was the first time that I sat in a car in the parking lot. We only lived a block from the church and school, so we always walked. But at my eighth-grade graduation, my mom was too sick from the chemo, so my father piled us all in the van and drove us the block to school. As we pulled into our spot, I looked around the parking lot and out at the horizon where the hills were in early May bloom. It was trippy to see a place that I had spent so much time look so different . . . just from viewing it from inside a car. Before I went into the graduation, my mother turned to me from the front seat, her bald head wrapped in a turban, her pointed finger and stern look focused on me, "When you go to the after party, no hokey pokey." That was it. That was the extent of my sexual education. Three words. "No. Hokey. Pokey."

I had no idea what she was talking about. But she seemed so fervent that I just nodded and agreed. "Sure! Yeah! No hokey pokey." I tried to decode her warning. But all I could think was, "You do the hokey pokey, and you turn yourself around, that's what it's all about!" Maybe my mom was trying to tell me to grow up and lay off the kids' games of tug-a-war and musical chairs and putting your left foot in and your left foot out. Those days were gone, I was headed to my first "boy/girl" party. This was no time for hokey pokey!

I gave her a meaningful and appreciative look back and agreed, "Okay, Mom. No hokey pokey."

The following May, I sat in another automobile in that same parking lot. This time it was a long black limo, and I imagined that this was what it would feel like to be a real live movie star. Then I joined my sisters in fogging up the windows. We watched silently as the pallbearers place our mom's coffin into the hearse, and sat back in our seats as our limo pulled out of the parking lot to join the funeral procession.

By late that same August, I fell in love with my first boyfriend Jason Claffy. We had met in summer school. He had a crooked smile and pale blue eyes and the ability to make me laugh when things were not-so funny. We sat at the top of Sorrows Hill and sipped whiskey from little bottles that he had stolen from his father's briefcase. We would stare out over the distant hill as it painted itself in shades of crimson and sunflower and blood orange mesmerized by its beauty and convinced that we lived in the most magnificent place on earth. I'm thinking the whisky had something to do with our conviction.

That October, we would meet at Sorrows Hill and spread a blanket on the grassy patch next to the lot and make out under the stars. Then we would go a little further, and a little further and further, until one night, curiosity killed the cat and we went all the way.

Right there on Sorrows Hill as I looked up to see the large cross staring down at me. "Oh no! I think we just did the hokey pokey. UckFay Eeemay."

I spent the next four years walking down the hill to take the train to Convent Station, where my sister Maggie and I went to high school at The Academy of St. Elizabeth.

Then I would take the train in the opposite direction into NYC to start my acting career. Soon after that, I was out seeing the world and had fewer and fewer reasons to visit Our Lady of Sorrows and her parking lot. On rare occasions like this, a wedding or family funeral or reunion, I could almost see the ghost of my past still running the yard, riding the Ferris wheel, fogging up windows, avoiding the hop-scotch, and sipping stolen whiskey.

In the aftermath of my life falling apart, I appreciated being back here on this lovely little spot of black gravel where I learned to sing and swear and fly and fuck.

Beth flipped on the radio, and we pulled out of the parking lot onto the street, leaving the memories in the rearview mirror.

"A hundred bucks a plate," Beth said. "That's not including the Venetian table for dessert. Plus, a hot air balloon that they'll take off in after the reception."

"A hundred bucks a plate." I repeated, hoping Beth wouldn't notice that I just revisited the conversation.

"Plus, a fucking hot air balloon!" Beth squawked as she blew smoke from her glossy lips out the car window.

"That's got to be an extra five grand right there. They're spending money like it's water. She didn't skimp on anything." Then Beth raised her voice to mimic Colleen.

"I'm only walking down the aisle once, and I'm going to do it right." I smiled at Beth's perfect impression. She should have come with me out to Hollywood. She was terrifyingly good, though I laughed at the idea that the amount of money you spent on a wedding could somehow act as marriage insurance.

What a good gig that would be, selling marriage insurance. But who would buy it? No one would think they needed, so even the most cautious wouldn't pay.

"Our marriage is different," they would say. "We're in it forever." Why would they get married at all if they didn't wholeheartedly believe that?

Beth's car sputtered its way up to the entrance of the gaudy castle, apparently "the place" to do it if you're going to do it right.

Maybe that was my problem. I had skimped on everything, from the wholesale flowers that I picked up in the Flower District of New York to asking my sisters to arrange them under the guise of some pre-wedding craft time. What kind of bullshit was that? I wore a borrowed dress and a second-hand headpiece, while our bands of gold were so plain and cheap they looked like a slice of copper pipe.

I should have realized when the best man came out of the kitchen armed with a broom and dustpan to clean up a plate of food he had accidentally dumped on the dance floor because they hadn't hired enough help. My marriage had the smell of failure from the start.

The cherry on top was that, somehow, someone on Reed's side of the family was related to Kevin Bacon. Yes, the six degrees of separation Kevin Bacon, so we ended up with The Bacon Brothers, a band made up of Kevin and his brother, to play at our reception.

All our wedding pictures, which were taken by my cousin, were of Reed and I standing in front of the band. Actually, they were pictures of Kevin with two blurry people in the foreground. The more I thought about it, the more foolish I felt for not seeing the signs. Our marriage was doomed from the start.

As we pulled up to the valet parking, I felt my energy drop to the floor.

"Are you okay?" Beth asked

"Yeah I guess, I'm just a little allergic to weddings I think." I added half-joking.

"At least you've been married," Pam offered. And for the first time, I felt a little guilty for my heartbreak.

"I feel like such a failure," I confessed.

"Well you're not. Is it a failed marriage when a woman who is abused finally leaves her husband?" She flipped her cigarette out the window and almost hit the valet.

"No, of course not," I mumbled. "But I haven't necessarily been abused, at least not physically, and I wasn't the one to leave. In fact, I wasn't even aware that there was a serious problem until I found the love letter in the set of keys. It's ridiculous how clueless I was, how embarrassing to be so typical."

"Well, don't worry Maureen. That's where the typicalness ends. I mean, who else can say they were left for Miss Universe? That's like comedy gold."

"Yeah, but I am not a comedian."

"Besides don't think of it as a loss. Sincerely, what did you lose? A husband who couldn't keep his dick in his pants? There's no value in that."

I smiled back at her, knowing she was right. After all was said and done, Miss Universe had inherited the uncomfortable role of having to consistently look over her shoulder. She would spend her hours fighting the urge to check his phone. She had won the right to a man whose words would always need to be carefully weighed, because in the end she had won a cheating man. And what a man will do to one, he will do to all. It's a very vain and stupid woman who falls for the idea that, "this time, it will be different."

The cocktail hour had always been my favorite, and this was no exception. Specialty drinks and artisan appetizers, and all those beautiful figures carved in ice, with the whole place draped in twinkle lights and pale pink peonies. It was magical. Everything was laid out so perfectly, the type of spread that made you feel guilty cutting into the liver pate molded in the shape of a dragonfly.

It was all the small talk that made me itchy. Pam already introduced me to way too many people who I knew I should have remembered. They all came with their own personal story of some very special and unforgettable time that we had all shared. I played along but honestly felt like Alice in Wonderland. I have always been terrible with names and faces, and the years of absence were not working in my favor.

I decided it was best to stay with the food and keep my back to the room. But first, one more glass of wine at the bar. I made eye contact with the bartender.

"Can I get a white wine?" I asked. His eyes lit up in recognition. *Oh no,* I thought. *Here we go again.*

"Hey, Lisa!" He smiled back at me.

I breathed a sigh of relief. "I am not Lisa," I said happily.

"No, I know, Maureen . . . I was calling you Lisa, from that commercial you were in.

What was it? Bud Light? You know, where the guy takes you out on a date, and then he takes you home, and you think that date is over, and then you like sneak back out to the bar, and he sees you there and he's like—" and, again, the bartender performed the same line as before— "Hey Lisa!" Then he looked at me and bowed a little and laughed. "Right, that was you, right?"

"Yep, that was me. I am Lisa, from the Bud Light commercial."

"Yeah, well, I'm trying to break into the business myself, you know," he announced after chopping some ice and handing me a white wine spritzer with a slice of lime. He had mixed up my order, but I didn't feel like renegotiating.

"Oh, really?" I was used to having this conversation. People came to me for Showbiz advice, for themselves or a really funny friend or talented daughter. They came to me like I had gone to Mickey Muldoon. It was the type of conversation I enjoyed and also that I could have on autopilot.

"Do you study anywhere?" I asked.

"Well, no," he answered still smiling. "But I watch a lot of day time soaps, and I've really learned a lot from that." He said it in such a sincere way that I almost laughed, until I realized he wasn't kidding.

"Well, that's great!" I managed after a pregnant pause. "But you should go ahead and enroll in a class. If for no other reason than to make a few connections." He reached in and patted my hand with a genuine smile of appreciation.

"Right on, thanks," he said as I stared back. I sucked up as much spritzer as my little red straw could handle. I was so jaded by the Hollywood scene that I was honestly unsure if he was being sinister or sincere.

This moment was moved on by the swelling sound of bagpipes and cake cutting and the best man making a drunken and rambling toast about how Colleen's husband had been with tons of broads, but that Colleen really was the best. Hands down. No contest.

Somehow, Pam and I managed to make it to the hot air balloon launch. Our stilettos sinking us into the grass as we hobbled our way over to see her off. We waved and cheered like drunken little munchkins to her Dorothy. I had survived the first wedding. Now I could survive anything.

～ TOOL ～

Show up and suit up. Life is not a dress rehearsal. We are not here to warm the bench. Every day we have the opportunity to take life on life's terms and find the good.

A spiritual vixen is visible, she shows up open hearted, open minded, and open handed. Holding her own and standing her ground. She is a solid temple of truth and authenticity. A well-lit lighthouse, she is not afraid of her own brilliance, and she always leaves her mark.

She is the one to count on in your darkest hour. She moves fast and carries little baggage. She shows up to tragedies and comedies with equal grace. She's quick to laugh and hard to ruffle. She is a gentle-hearted warrior who is unfazed about the arrival of her own tears or anger. She lets them come like clouds, knowing they will be honored and then pass. Her truth is sharp and clear and able to cut through the bull shizzle like a hot knife through butter. She smacks you with just enough truth to make you get back up. She may not know exactly where she's going, but she always shows up to where she is supposed to be. She has an unflinching and unapologetic faith in the grand plan of the Divine. She arrives without shame, blame, or guilt, dressed in a conqueror smile and a killer pair of stilettos.

～ DO THIS ～

Make a commitment to show up. Sure, there will be a million reasons to stay home in the sweatpants and pass on the wedding invitations. But when you show up for others, you are also blessed. So, go to the weddings, funerals, baby blessings, and birthday parties. Even if it's just an appearance. Magic happens when you show up.

Remember showing up is not the same as showing off. One is done for the highest good of all and the other is done for the ego. When you show up, you show the world what is important to you. You are investing with your most valuable resource, your time.

Chapter 8

Tell Your Stories

Miracles are healing because they supply a lack;
they are performed by those who temporarilty have
more for those who temporarily have less.
—ACIM

The next day I arrived a bit hungover and haggered to the train station in South Orange. Beth and I had stayed up to the wee hours catching up, toasting the bride and the groom—and anyone else deserving of a toast. Turns out there were many toast-worthy souls.

My head was throbbing as I made my way up the stairs to the platform. I would take the train to Hoboken, then jump on the Path train to New York and meet up with Alexi at the White Horse Tavern. He had offered to give me a ride to LaGuardia airport to catch my flight back to Los Angeles.

I found a spot on the platform where I could see South Orange Avenue with its shops and steeples. I watched the traffic snake its way up South Orange Avenue towards the lush green hills that had been the backdrop of my childhood. This place, this town, and this station were the springboard that I had leaped from. I took it all in and felt a deep reverence for the simple, small town, sweetness and stability. I was a daughter of the community no matter how far I flew, and she would always be here holding space for me.

As I stared out at the horizon I noticed a young mom making her way up the stair carrying a baby stroller. I went over and grabbed an end to assist her with the last few steps. This act of kindness had been shown to me a million times when I lived in Sunnyside Queens and as I traveled the city on the subway.

The people who had helped me never asked permission. They just reached in and grabbed an end. It was an unspoken tribal agreement. But for some reason on this day, being on the other end of the carriage, something was triggered and I could feel my emotions rise. I rested the carriage safely on the plateform. She whispered a thanks and I exhaled a breath I had not known that I was holding. It was an exhale to the inhale I had taken when I first found out I was pregnant. The inhale that got stuck in my fear that I would be doing this motherhood thing on my own. But in that moment, on the other end of a stranger's carriage, I got to see how wrong I had been. When I said yes to motherhood, little did I know then that a million midwives were called to duty, some would show up to hold a door, or grab an end of a stoller, or hold your hand as they walked a while with you 'till you found your own footing. I had been running on the illusion that motherhood was a solo gig, when all along it had been communal.

The old train pulled into the station and the conductors stepped onto the platform as we boarded. I took a seat and stared out the window as the car bucked, and then we rolled into motion. Pulling away from my hometown made me long for my own mother.

It had been over ten years that she had passed, but the wound had not completely healed. She was diagnosed when I was nine and died a few short years later when I was fourteen. It was one of those cancers that seemed to come and go, leaving just enough hope with its departure to ensure that it be powerfully painful on its return. It was really the chemotherapy that made her health rise and fall like a baby learning to walk.

My mother was a religious woman who had given birth to eight children and kept the door open for anyone who needed a warm meal or a place to sleep. We lived a block from the Church, and she was down there praying every day, rain or shine. It was a peaceful sanctuary, compared to our loud and busy over populated home. She loved to pray, did so as if Jesus and Mary were her close personal friends.

When she wasn't saying prayers, she would write them on loose papers, and the back of envelopes and on slightly used napkins that she left around the house. Then as if that were not enough, after dinner each evening, she would have us all say the Rosary together.

As her disease progressed, my mother began to be inundated by alternative healers. The whole community knew and loved our mom, and when it became apparent that the chemo and radiation were not doing the trick, folks began making suggestions.

"Joni, try these herbs."

"Joni, you should drink these vitamin shakes."

"Joni, I heard about a lady who gets messages from Jesus, maybe she can heal you."

Almost every day, a well-intended friend would show up at the door with a suggestion for a new treatment. The recommendations came with a newsletter or pamphlet, citing cures and healings, and testimonials that would suck us all in. Nothing was too woo-woo, no rock would be unturned.

There was Virginia, from Brooklyn, who saw the face of Jesus in her windowpane; and Rita, from Queens, who sold water blessed by her visions of the Virgin Mother. Along with the chemo, my mother willingly tried oils, tonics, and trips to holy healers to see if they might help prolong her life and hold back the cancer that was encroaching upon it.

I read through them all looking for a miracle, but one of those newsletters caught my attention. This particular newsletter had an article about these children in Medjugorje, Yugoslavia, who were being visited by apparitions of the Blessed Mother.

The article explained how the Blessed Mother was appearing to these kids, giving them messages, sending healing, and causing miracles. I was completely intrigued. I loved the Blessed Mary; I loved hearing my mother's stories about Mary's intercessions and her ability to grant miracles. Every time I saw a statue of The Blessed Mother, I felt drawn in. Even her statues emanated such beauty and peace.

All my genuflecting to the Blessed Mother and decorating altars to her with stolen flowers from our neighbor's yard, all the little answered prayers that I had credited her with, had established a sweet and confident faith within me. While in church, the beautiful statues of the Blessed Mother were always a welcomed distraction from having to look up at the bloody Jesus on the cross. No offense to Jesus but they caught him at his worst hour. Really what was the thinking there?

When I read the article on our dining room table about the Children of Medjugorje, and how they were witnessing healings I felt a powerful longing and thought, *I want to go there.* When I read that it was located in Yugoslavia, and that Yugoslavia was across the ocean and around the world, I laid the newsletter down on the table, and with it I let go of any hope of a healing.

Going to Yugoslavia seemed as possible as going to Mars. Aside from my wild, world traveling Aunt Julia, I didn't know anyone who went anywhere. Sure, my parents went on a cruise once, and my mom would go on a trip to Ireland before she died, but these were special trips. As far as I could see, if you lived in New Jersey, you stayed in New Jersey. We had New York City for our entertainment and the Jersey shore for our vacations. Nobody just flew off to Yugoslavia.

Anyhow, I was not fully convinced that a trip to Medjugorje would have held back the impending nature of my mother's death. That train was coming, I could feel the rumble, and when it did arrive there would be no escape. My siblings and I were all pennies on the track, destined to be squashed and flattened.

The pain of the heartbreak was debilitating, and I had no real safe haven to express it. So I dealt with the pain the way that I had seen adults deal with their pain: alcohol.

Alcohol was our cure all. When you had a sore tooth, you got a little whiskey on the gums; if you had a cold, a hot toddy would do the trick; and although there was not a cure for a broken heart, you were welcomed to drink yourself silly trying to find it.

Within the year, my father got remarried to a woman who had never been married and had no kids. She had imagined *Eight is Enough*, but what she got was *The Amityville Horror*. A house filled with eight angry teenagers who were mourning their mother.

I graduated high school, and instead of college, I took a lateral move. I just needed a place to nurse my wounds, a gap year.

"I am going to travel, maybe learn a new language, find myself and my passion." I suggested to my counselor at the college prep-high school that I was going to. I am sure he could see right through me. Upon graduation, I effectively packed up my stuff and shacked up with my friend Bebe whose family lived a few blocks away, and I started a sincere relationship with alcohol. So much for travel and new languages.

If my pain was fire, alcohol was gasoline. My unexpressed sadness had fermented in my gut and turned to rage, and my rage had turned to self-sabotage. My life was a pointless cycle of waking up late, watching soap operas, smoking cigarettes with Bebe's older brother Ken, who was an artist and musician, and then heading to work. After work, I would hang out with friends, drink, and fool around with any miscellaneous man available and then drink some more till I passed out. Then I would wake the next morning feeling terrible about myself. But the only thing that I had to take the edge off was alcohol, so the next night I would just drink more.

The good news was that I was a fun drunk. With a little alcohol, I was a liquid linguist of lore and logic. I could converse on anything. Alcohol was my truth serum, my capsule of courage, barleycorn of bravery. Suddenly I was winning friends and influencing people. I mean, not really, but in my drunk mind I was the shit. I was one of those people who, when drunk, could convince lots of people to do stupid things. It was sort of a gift.

I was one-part sermon two-parts stand up, and as the night poured out I was a dash of stutter with a reverence for repeating myself. But it was all good. Alcohol was my loyal wingman who helped me to fly with the philosophers. A person can get addicted to a friend like that.

Before long and with the help of Bebe's mom, I found my way to a dark smoky basement. A secret society of sober storytellers, otherwise known as Alcoholics Anonymous. I was barely eighteen years old, not even old enough to legally drink, and yet coming to the realization that maybe I never could.

I connected with a sponsor named Ronda B. She was a wiry like a Whippet and worn like an old shoe. But she was one of the most grateful people I had ever met. Instead of the *Big Book of AA*, she gave me her dogeared copies of Louis Hays, *You Can Heal Your Life* and *The Greatest Salesman in the World: Og Mandino*. I stayed somber long enough to read them. Every page of these books blew my mind. Since I was no longer hanging out at the bars after work, I would sit up at night poring through the pages of these books. They left me in complete awe and wonder. I was dazed that there were others out there on this big blue marble who thought like me.

As breathtaking a vantage point that Ronda and her self-help library offered, I could not honestly imagine life without alcohol. Alcohol was my family's bloodline. It was the river that ran through every conversation. Although it didn't mend my broken heart, it dulled the pain enough for me to journey on. At least temporarily.

At Mountain Station our train jerked and pulled to a stop. The car doors opened and a conductor made his way down the aisle clicking his ticket punch.

"Get your tickets out," he called. I reached into my bag and found my ticket and a sample packet of aspirin. I clipped my ticket to the seat in front of me, popped the pills dry, and turned my gaze back out the window. Just in time to catch a glimpse of the little community theatre where I did my first play.

I got the part while living at Bebe's house, her other older brother Ken cast me in a community production of *Bus Stop* to play the Marilyn Monroe part. The experience was terrifying. I wore a dress covered in sequins and crystals that seemed to jingle and jangle all on its own. Each night that I made it out on the stage, I was a jitter sparkly mess. My lines came out faint and robotic, every prop that I picked up sent my hand vibrating. My nervousness was so distracting that my poor scene partner practically had to hold me down.

Community theater people are some of the most forgiving people in the world. The cast did not give up on me, and one night, a few weeks into the run, my nerves settled, and the words began to make their way out in a way that was surprisingly aligned with my character's motivation. I learned to act the way some kids learn to swim. Tossed in the deep end and fearfully wrestling with the water for air.

After that one magical performance, there was no going back. I had found my voice, my stroke, my style. It did not come like a sunrise, easy and gentle. It came like an honest old man with no Viagra. Jagged and jumpy and awkward and earnest. But it came. And when it comes like that, there is so much more to appreciate about it.

It was on that little stage in that beaded dress that I fell head over heels in love with acting and the delightful escape that it offered. Once bit by the acting bug, my sights were set on New York.

This train was the white chariot that delivered me to the Big Apple a couple times a week. I auditioned for the American Academy of Dramatic Arts, encouraged by my triumph in community theater. With one play under my belt and a head filled with promises from Louise Hay's book, I affirmed my way into being accepted. "I have within me all the ingredients for success," I whispered before launching into my audition monologues.

The letter of acceptance was a prized possession. Thanks to a loan from my sister Mary, I enrolled in the summer program and got signed by an agent and booked my third audition. Next thing I knew, I was flying first class to Tennessee to shoot a series of Pepsi commercials. I was clueless. When they handed me a week of per diem I thought they were paying me in cash.

I started working regularly in stage and film. Though the heartbreak and pain that I felt were not something that we talked about at home, as an actress I could express all of it. Every last drop of the pain and sadness that I had stored up could be used, and I could get paid for it. So that was a healthy win-win.

Although my priest dreams had gone dormant, the work that I was doing felt inspired. I was on stage, sharing the truth and telling stories, making people laugh and cry and connect. I didn't need anyone's permission or different body parts for that, and my efforts were met with applause and creative fulfillment. I became so immersed in my craft that I gave up almost everything else. It was like I had unknowingly taken a vow of poverty—because I was definitely a starving artist—and chastity—I was so busy working, creating, and funneling my energy into my craft that I had no time for romance. I am sure this single focus passion curbed my alcohol consumption as well. I am pretty sure that acting saved my life. Those early years of my career were lean and lovely times.

The train made its final stop in Hoboken and I looked up to see the other travelers moving into the center aisle. I grabbed my bags and moved into line.

The Hoboken train station always made me feel like I was on a movie set. The high ceilings and rich wooden benches, the walls echoed with a million stories to tell, but I had no time to sit and listen.

Alexi was already waiting at the entrance of the White Horse Tavern. He swung me in the air in a full bear hug. The years since we had last seen each other had aged him in a favorable way. His frumpy fashion suggested that his hard earned success had allowed him some casual privilege. His unshaven face stretched with his signature smile. The same one that was once used to scalp tickets was now being put to use seducing jurors.

"Did you go by HB?" he asked as we found our way to a table. I shook my head no and tried to keep up with him.

"I saw Jasmine in an episode of Seinfeld," he shot over his shoulder as he settled into a booth.

"Really?"

"And Simon, do you remember Simon?"

"Yeah, of course, tall Simon, he was really good."

"Yeah, he waits tables at some diner in midtown."

"Really?"

"I know it makes no sense, your business is brutal and has you all brainwashed. I offered Simon a job working for me and he turned me down," Alexi laughed.

"Acting is a jealous lover, she wants us all to herself," I offered. He shook his head and waved the waitress over.

Alexi and I first met at HB studios in a scene study class led by Herbert Bergdorf himself. Alexi was in law school at the time and had no intention of being an actor. He was taking Herbert's class to gain confidence in public speaking and become a better attorney.

All these years later, it seemed the investment had paid off. Alexi had strategically climbed each rung of the ladder. As much as he liked to ridicule the entertainment industry, he sure liked to reminisce about his time on stage with the thespians.

"Remember when we did that scene together where we botched the whole thing and started just improvising lines?" His eyes lit up with the memory.

"We had no business being on stage," I laughed. "We were both so insanely nervous that when we skipped a few lines and got all turned around, neither of us let on."

"You just kept repeating the same thing over and over."

"It was an artistic choice!" I defended. "And he loved it!" I laughed

"Yeah, he did." Alexi's smile grew even brighter.

"I remember looking over at you like we had just got done with a crazy roller coaster ride," I smiled.

"Then he showered us with praise. And we sat there trying to play it cool as if we had a clue as to what had just happened."

I stared across the table at Alexi reliving that moment feeling once again like two street kids who had snuck into a movie and, had somehow gone undetected. I was reminded why we had become fast friends.

At the time Alexi was paying for his tuition and putting himself through school by scalping tickets. To insure that he didn't jeopardize his legal standings, he asked me to attend every concert with him and hold the money. I was basically his money mule, which I had no problem with. I sat front row at the Rolling Stones, Elton John, Billy Joel and any one else who played Madison Square garden or Radio City Music Hall. All I had to do was carry the cash. Never once did I think, *"I could get in trouble for this."* I just thought, *"I am helping out a friend."* It felt powerful to sit front row and walk around with thousands of dollars in my pocket.

It was great getting caught up. After a couple drinks and a lot of laughs he drove me to the airport. As we said good-bye in the car, he reached into his back seat and grabbed a package.

"I've been wanting to give this to you," he said and placed it on my lap.

"What is this?"

"Open it on the plane. It will give you something to do on the flight."

"I hope it's not a bomb," I said smiling.

"You have a dark mind. You know that, right?" He reached over and gave me a hug goodbye.

I had an hour before boarding so I grabbed a seat at an

airport bar and opened the package because I am terribly impatient and it would not be the first time that Alexi had me smuggle something illegal.

I pulled away the wrapping and found a huge photo album filled with pictures of our trip to Medjugorje. As I flipped through the pages so many memories poured out. He was right; this would keep me busy on the flight. That trip to Medjugorje and his friendship had all gone so unappreciated at the time.

The trip came a year after us "working" together, he told me he was taking his mom to Russia for a vacation, because that was where she was from.

"Of course I am going to smuggle in some American Levi jeans, and smuggle out some Russian Samovars." He pointed this out as if it was the standard thing that happened when visiting Russia.

"Of course," I joked.

"Then we are were planning a stop in Medjugorje, Yugoslavia. My mother wants to see some kids . . . something about the Blessed Mother—"

"I know about Medjugorje!" I cut him off. "I can't believe you are going there. I have always wanted to see that."

"Really? You should come with us"

"I would love to, but I don't have the money for that."

"What if I paid for you?"

"Seriously? What if I never paid you back?" Alexi just laughed.

"It's not problem, I can pay for you," he offered.

"Seriously Alexi, I may never pay you back," I confessed, honestly overwhelmed by his generosity.

"That's fine," He shrugged.

"Seriously? I am going to Medjugorje?" I jumped up from the table and ran around the room with my hands in the air.

I loved getting to see all the pictures from our time in Russia and Yugoslavia. Alexi and I knew how to get our drink on together. The waitress strolled by and I ordered a vodka to add a little flavor to the trip down memory lane.

The crazy thing was that at the very same time that Alexi had invited me to Yugoslavia, Sylvia Leigh, my tiara touting acting guru and Barbara Garret, my manager, were getting ready to send a handful of young adults out to Los Angeles for pilot season. Their plan was that this select tribe of talent would head off to the Hollywood, nab a few TV credits, and return to New York with a bit more confidence and fatter resumes.

Pilot season is always a busy time for actors, and a good time to be in Los Angeles. I didn't have the money to join the group of actors going to LA, but to my surprise these two women came to me and said, "We are going to pay your way to LA. You will book work there, and pay us back." It was less of an invitation and more of a demand. Barbara Garrett really believed in me and took it upon herself to guilt Sylvia into the agreement.

"You're always telling me how great she is, why don't we go in on her ticket together?"

They had so much confidence and faith in me, I could not turn down their offer.

I remember feeling like there was a plan in action that I was not fully aware of. Things were unfolding, and although they were for the most part good, they were definitely not experiences that I would have ever even known to ask for. It was like I was Cinderella, heading to the ball all on the generosity of a million fairy godmothers.

What it came down to was that I would spend two months in Los Angeles, where I would basically be pseudo in charge of about six underaged kids ranging from thirteen to sixteen. I was the adult by default. I was the oldest, but definitely not the most mature. After this tour of duty, I would fly home to New York just in time to board the plane with Alexi and his mom. For a girl who didn't think she would make it out of New Jersey, I was suddenly becoming a world traveler.

I arrived in Los Angeles for pilot season for the first time with a small tribe of lost boys and girls looking to cut their teeth on stardom. The seven of us shacked up at the Barham Apartments in Burbank. The other kids came from privileged families. They would party hard all night, sleep in late, and wait by the pool for our agent to call. I was not as lucky. I spent the mornings working at Barney's Beanery with a staff of well-seasoned professional waitresses who were all within the average age of sixty. These ladies were in no way interested in showing me the ropes. The clientele at Barney's was young Hollywood grunge. I made my rent in nickels and dimes, and tried not to smell of hamburgers and cigarettes when I was sent straight from work to an audition. Every once in a while, Johnny Depp would come in with his manager and sit at my table. He would keep his sad eyes to the table, and she would instruct me, "Don't mess things up because we have an important meeting." Then Johnny would whisper his order to me, and I would dream about the day that he and I would go riding off into the sunset. But that never happened. I always thought that the manager gave me way more power than necessary. To think that my messing up an order would have any impact on Johnny's career was generous.

It was during my last week in LA that I booked a role on the show *Tour of Duty*. I played Dolly, the southern sweetheart who gets dumped by her boyfriend played by Kyle Chandler. Kyle was great to work with. Dolly was only being dumped because Kyle's character had come home from war blind, and he did not want to subject Dolly to a life of being married to a blind man. It was a sweet and emotional scene, and I felt like I was inches from true fame. This is a normal illusion that settles on every actor like a good hand at a poker table. "This is it!" we want to scream. "It's my time!" But more important than impending fame was the fact that, with the money from that one job, I was able to pay back my agent and manager, and even keep some for myself.

Thanks to being roomates with Skye, I would rub elbows with all kinds of celebrities and artists. But it was our last week in LA, when she introduced me to a group of her college friends that would change the trajectory of my life. They had driven out from Tucson, Arizona, and I can't remember the connection that they had with Skye, friends or friends of friends.

She told the guys that we would meet them at the top of Mulholland Drive's scenic overlook. Just to keep it interesting, I drove us to the top of Mulholland and we parked.

"Let me get in the driver seat so they think I drove?" Skye asked. She was a sixteen-year-old city kid. She had yet to get a license, and thanks to New York's great public transportation, probably never would.

"Sure," I agreed.

We switched places and waited for them to arrive.

"Tell me a story," she insisted. "You're a really good story-teller. Tell me the one about you and your siblings going down the hill in the shopping cart."

I was twenty-two years old, and this was the first time that anyone had ever asked me to tell a story or say I was a "good storyteller." So that in itself would have been enough foreplay to have me weaving webs for hours. But the real beauty of the comment was that it came from her. Skye, the Pied Piper of poetry and culture and art. That is the magic of a good friend, someone who sees in you something that had gone unnoticed and unwit-nessed, and they casually reach in to your oyster, gather your pearls, and present them back to you.

That day, on the hilltop of Mulholland, all the world faded as I performed a story for my grateful audience of one, complete with dips and turns and traps and escapes. I could have sat spinning tales forever, immersed in this new awareness that I was a "good storyteller."

When they arrived, Skye got so excited that the risky rendezvous had worked that she jumped out of the car. I got out on my side, and Skye slammed the door shut, locking the car with the keys inside.

It was Dean, a fair-haired Tom Cruise look alike, who was able to retrieve the keys with a wire hanger. The rest of the guys called Dean "MacGyver." Dean and I had a connection that felt magnetic, I am not sure that I felt that way with anyone before or since. It was not just sexual, we hardly even spoke. We were two of the most awkward people to be around.

But before the week was up, I had somehow invited him to come to New York and try his hand at acting. I had suggested that he could live with me and my roommate, Mina. Dean and I had not even kissed, and I was convincing him to shed his life and move to the Big Apple. It was right after the movie *Dead Poets Society* had come out, and we were all high on the fumes of carpe diem.

As the guys loaded their car to drive back to Arizona, Dean asked me to write something romantic on a piece of paper. I grabbed his pen and jotted something down and begged him not to look at it until he was out of California. Skye and I waved them off as she asked what I had written.

"I just wrote the words, 'something romantic'," I confessed, and it sent the two of us laughing like hillbillies.

The next day, we made our way back to New York. Skye headed back to high school, and I arrived in time to catch a plane with Alexi to Europe.

Thinking back on this time in my life, when everything seemed to line up in perfect order, even when it seemed so chaotic and unplanned, gave me a certain splash of hope as I boarded the plan back to Los Angeles.

— TOOL —

You can plaster the world with promotions and pleas, or you can seduce the world with a story and song. There is no better craft to help you succeed than the art of telling a good story. If you are ready to be truly visible, it's time to harvest your stories,

Storytelling has been the single most powerful tool that I use to cause and create community, content, and prosperity. My love for stories started as a young child surrounded by a tribe of Irish storytellers.

Storytelling is good for the soul, the family, the community, the love-life, and the business. Basically, being a better storyteller will improve every area of your life. It's a powerful way to heal as well as reveal your truth. It's also a great way to connect with clients. We all have something to say and share that needs to be expressed.

— DO THIS —

Start to notice all the places that stories are around you—stories of your family, your friends, on TV, in the media, Facebook, the news, movies. It's all stories. Begin to think about the three most impactful stories that have changed your life. Write them out and practice telling them. Even if you share them alone in your car, or to an audience of one in front of your bathroom mirror. Just start. Tell your stories.

Don't fear the truth, the more you practice the more comfortable you will become with the sound of your own voice. Tell it like it is, use all the words you need. Don't worry about your words being pretty, or perfect or poetic. Use words in creative, unconventional, and controversial ways. Don't water down, sugar coat, or parcel out your truth. If you need to make a point, use sharp words. If the truth makes you stutter, sweat or cry . . . so be it. Don't let your fear of exposure prevent you from delivering the truth. Sometimes deliveries are messy. If your content is true they will forget the mess and remember the message. And if given the opportunity, write "something romantic."

Chapter 9

Ask Questions

To give and to receive are one in Truth.
—A Course in Miracles

O n the flight back to Los Angeles, I took my time going through the photo album. The trip to Yugoslavia happened before I got pregnant, before Reed, before everything. It happened at a time in my life when I had no idea about the major changes that were right beyond the horizon. So much had changed since that trip, but as I flipped through the pages the whole experience came flooding back as if it was yesterday.

We landed in Yugoslavia after a long flight, and we took a two-hour bumpy cab ride from the airport to Medjugorje. Alexi, his mom, me, and a couple of very large suitcases. I was not then, nor have I ever been, a very smart packer.

We stayed with local families and spent our days visiting the church and various locations where the children shared the message of the Blessed Mother. In the center of town was the largest church I had ever seen. It was called St. James, after the Patron Saint of Pilgrims, though it made me feel anything but welcomed. It was massive and intimidating and looked so out of place in the middle of this small farm town.

We got tucked into the local home where we were staying and made plans to hike up one of the hills where we would all pray together, and the children would share the messages of the Blessed Mother with us. By this point, the original children were actually young adults, but they were still experiencing visits from the Blessed Mother, and they would speak and answer questions.

The first night was magical as we hiked up the side of this large hill. Arriving at the top, we were greeted by an amazing sight. Hundreds of people from all corners of the world saying the Rosary together. The moon was bright and under a deep, blue sky and a million stars, I knelt and joined them in prayer. There was something so mystical about being in a foreign country on a hillside, with hundreds of voices praying the same prayer in so many different languages. I felt as though we were weaving a prayer with our words, coming together on the common ground of faith.

I closed my eyes and listened to all the voices melding together into one holy hymn, like we had found a bridge that connected us. The sounds swirled around me and forced me to open my eyes. I just needed to take it all in. To really see this beautiful and diverse demonstration of holy communion. I knew that I was supposed to be bowing my head and staying on track with the call and response of the prayer. However, I could not close myself off from this moment and this crowd of people, lit only by moonlight, kneeling in prayer on top of a mountain in Yugoslavia. It will forever be etched in my mind as a view of what peace on earth looked like.

After the prayers were done, one of the children began to talk about the messages he received from the Blessed Mother. He told us that, when he was done, we were allowed to ask questions.

Questions! Well of course I had a few of those, but at this point I was a little shy about asking. I felt like I had been shut down when it came to asking spiritual questions.

On this particular night, the message was that Mary was weeping over the fact that we were *"throwing away our children."* She pleaded with us to pray. This went on for a while. The Blessed Mother was weeping over this, and the Blessed Mother was weeping over that. It felt just like more of the same Catholic guilt trip that I had endured my entire life. I felt myself getting agitated and depressed. All the talk about Mary weeping felt draining. I had never thought of her as a weeper, except of course at the crucifixion. Aside from that little hiccup, she always seemed so serene. After all, she was billed as "the Queen of Peace." How could the Queen of Peace be involved in so much drama and distress?

Suddenly I felt a question spring to mind and begin to boil to the surface. As much as I tried to keep a lid on it, it would not be contained. I fought back by reminding myself about all the times my questions had gotten me in trouble. I reasoned that even if I did ask my question, the answers never satisfied. I did this in the hopes that I would be strong enough not to let my curiosities win. Yet this question was an itch that would not be denied. While I didn't want to have the children frown on me or, worse yet, shut me down with accusations of "being too bold," I also realized that I could not stop myself. I watched my hand go up, and then to my horror and surprise, they called on me. Almost against my will, my body stood and before I could even begin to formulate the question, it flew from my lips.

"You talk a great deal about the Blessed Mother weeping, and I was just wondering, does she ever laugh, and if so what makes her happy?"

The clarity of the words surprised me, as I stood there open and vulnerable in the moonlight waiting to be shot down.

I could tell my question had caused a stir as few heads turned to see who the town idiot was who would ask such a thing. The young man who had called on me brought his hand to his chin and began rubbing it thoughtfully as he leaned back on his heels.

He began speaking, but it all sounded like babble. I didn't understand a word of it. As my focus pulled from him, I was suddenly aware of an older lady kneeling next to me. She was roughly a billion years old and wore a black lace prayer shawl on her head. Her hands were up by her mouth and clasped in prayer, her knuckles old and knobby, her eyebrows bushy and expressive. She looked a bit grumpy, like she had been praying for years with no answers. She caught my eye, and for a second, I felt her look at me in the way the nuns had looked at me back in school. Before I could look away, she leaned in and whispered three words, "Good question, honey." Then she bobbed her head and smiled ever so slightly to let me know she was sincere.

As you can imagine, this exchange just about knocked me on my ass, and it took me a while to fully digest her words. *Good question honey? Me?* Then right there on that holy hill in Yugoslavia, I had a healing. Something dropped away from me, something that I did not need to retrieve.

I stared down at her bright and beautiful face looking up at me, her kind words echoed in my soul. "Good question, honey." I slowly knelt back down, grateful to meld back in with the fold. As I bowed my head, a smile spread from ear to ear. Me, the-good-question asker: who would have guessed?

Good question, honey was like hearing angels sing. To this day, if someone approaches me with a question of any sort, I like to pay them forward. "Good question," I say. I have taken to dropping the word "honey" because I am not a billion yet.

"Good question, honey," were three of the kindest words I had ever received and worth every bumpy, dusty mile to Yugoslavia. Little did I know the blessings had only begun.

The very next evening, we hiked back up the hill, and again we were met with a large crowd of people praying the Rosary, all in different languages. I don't remember the message that night, but I remember a man in front asking a very interesting question.

"Aside from the bible, what books did Mary recommend?" Now, to be completely honest with you, at the time I thought it was the stupidest question that ever was. I could not imagine Mary reading a book. It felt like he was asking, "Does Mary take cream in her tea?" But since I was a newly recovering *bad-question-asker*, I tried my best to let it slide. What surprised me was that the children had an answer for his question.

"Mary says there are two psychotherapists in New York City who are doing some very good work, and they have written a book with her son called *Song of Prayer*." I was mesmerized and confused by this response. First off, I actually thought, *Who is her son?* Then I was like, *Wait, what? Jesus is writing a book?* This was the strangest idea I had ever heard. Why would he write a book with psychotherapists? Why would he write a book at all?

I supposed His writing a book is as acceptable as Mary showing up to converse with some children in Yugoslavia. None of it really made sense.

The final thing I thought was, *I live in New York! I am going to find that book.* I made a silent vow that once I got back to the States, I would go hunting for these two psychotherapists or at least their book, and see what all the "to do" was about. Keep in mind that this was before cell phones, Google, and the Internet, so I sat on that hill and willed myself to remember the name of the book, *Song of Prayer, Song of Prayer,* I must remember *Song of Prayer.* I committed myself to searching for it as soon as possible.

A funny thing happens when you make plans. So, what actually happened was that when I got back to New York, Dean aka MacGuyver arrived and moved in with me and Mina. We had the shortest of relationships, less than two weeks. As it turned out, I never did have to bring up the conversation with

Mina about having an extra roommate because he was there for a little more than a week before we realized that we were completely incompatible. In the end it was not actually "something romatic" at all.

He moved out, but not before I got pregnant. So that happened and suddenly, chasing down the Blessed Mother's suggested reading list was the least of my worries. He was not ready to be a father, and I was not ready to drag some extra weight around, so I let him go his way.

I was not the first woman to walk through this moment. I had many friends and family members who found themselves with an unplanned pregnancy. I saw the path and knew my options. There were many ahead of me who had chosen abortion and a few who sided with adoption, but at the time, I had no role models for being a single parent. No one I knew chose this when given the choice.

I am not sure if it was the echo of Mary's weeping, or the guilt-inducing glares of the nuns at school, or if it was just my own romantic idea of motherhood and my rebel spirit that fired me into motivation every time I heard the word, "No." It may have been a combination of all of it, but the sum total was that I was keeping the baby and raising it on my own.

When I told my coach and manager, they were both pretty shocked and sad. They had just invested in me and, although they didn't say it, I felt like I had let them down. They suggested that I not keep the baby, that it would be a career killer. But I had made my mind up about these things long before the news arrived. I may not have been fully equipped to be a great parent, but I also was not afraid of it. I was young, yes, but I was not a teenager. I was a young adult. I could handle this.

I was a cockeyed optimist and a romantic rebel. I would have this baby and have my life. I made a conscious promise that I would not lose my cool over this. I was making this promise for my entire being. I was not willing to surrender or sacrifice my essence to crawl into some confining cocoon of maternity wear and the limited ideas that came with it. A mother is supposed to look like this and act like that and be . . . motherly. I was not buying it.

I will make motherhood hip, I thought to myself.

This was prior to the shift in the social awareness that pregnant women did not need to hide their baby bumps, and even before there was any real variety in fashion choices outside of a floral-printed tent dresses with the Peter Pan collar. These fashion options were dismal, and yet a brilliant way to ensure that pregnant woman felt ridiculous. To shame the body for doing the most beautiful thing possible, carrying a life. It was unthinkable to imagine feeling sexy or attractive, and yet I never felt more beautiful and vibrant in my life, especially in the early months of pregnancy.

I was not willing to surrender to the social agreements of motherhood. I tried on the maternity wear that was lent to me by sisters and friends. I looked in the mirror and felt like a circus clown. It was like I was back in Catholic school and being asked to wear a uniform again,

"One tent fits all." My nonconformist spirit wanted none of it. I was having a baby, this was not a deformity needing a camouflage. I would not be hiding. I was on the early cusp of the celebrity pregnancy boom, prior to the days when Demi Moore showed up on Vanity Fair in nothing but her birthday suit.

I was told by my team to not mention the pregnancy until I had to. It was to be shrouded in secrecy. You could be a starlet or a mother but not both.

Well, I wasn't so sure about that. I wanted both.

Sure, I would need to take a sabbatical, but I would be an example of possibility. I remember this being a conscious choice.

There were a lot of things that would be affected because of this choice. I was cast in a movie trailer opposite Sandra Bullock, and the director had gotten the backing to make the movie. I needed to bow out. My window of working was closing fast. In my first trimester, I was on *As the World Turns* in a bikini and no one knew a thing. But soon after that things dried up. There are not many parts for pregnant ingenues.

It was hard to see all my young fabulous friends on the fast track to fame. As each day passed, the romance wore off. My loyal fan club of Sylvia and Barbara had turned their attention to the next pretty ingenue positioned for fame. My truth began to get painfully clear. I called my dad, and he came and helped me move back to New Jersey. But I made a promise to myself, this was temporary, and I would be back. I rented my old place back from my sister and set up a sweet sanctuary to bring my baby home to.

I painted the little room that once held all my shoes and borrowed a crib. I also received a donated glider and a sweet little shelf that held lotions and powder and baby books. And, although this child was not planned, I let it know with every breath that it was wanted.

I would lay on my bed and rub my belly and imagine my child's heartbeat. I went through a million names and a thousand baby books. It was like I was having a secret affair with a child that I had yet to meet, and I was unapologetically fearless when asked.

"Yes, I am pregnant and yes, I am having it on my own." This was usually met with shock or pity, but I was determined not to let those limited ideas brand me.

Although I was putting up a good front, I was in fear for my future and my ability to be a good mom. I am sure that these feelings are natural, but for a single mother they are multiplied.

The world looked in at me with a sorrowful gaze: *What are you going to do? What will become of you?* I felt like I was treading water and scanning the horizon for a lifeboat. The truth was I did not want to do this by myself, but I didn't see another way.

That was when Reed showed up with his pesky questions about whether I was wearing a new bra and his promises that he would walk with me through this chapter. He stood like a modern-day Joseph to my Mary.

I think the detour came when I fell asleep to his promises, to what he represented. Did I fall in love with him? Yes. Did I need someone to walk me through anything? I am not so sure about that. I think that was where I abandoned myself. I abandoned my sweet little baby room that I worked so hard on creating. I moved to Queens with Owen, and I became a wife when I was only be asked to be a mother.

Here I was four years later, on a plane back to LA, finally taking an inventory of how I had abandoned myself and taken a detour. It was a handsome and helpful and husbandly type of detour. But a detour all the same.

It was fear that had me flee to Reed's apartment in Queens, as much as I hated to admit it. But in that reckoning, something had come clear. Something confusing had come back into focus. There was a longing for my own authentic spiritual connection that was not laced with myths and laden with dogma. Something had reawakened in me, a thought that had gone dormant. And now that I had a clear canvas, a semi clear head, and a few months left on my sex sabbatical, maybe this was the time to let myself return to that well-rooted woman who had not surrendered her script to play the role that society saw as more fitting. Maybe this would be the time that I let myself ask the harder questions, and follow my own truth without compromise or apology.

⌒ TOOL ⌒

Ask questions. Questions are the springboard to creativity and inventions.

You never know where your answers live 'till you ask the question.

The universe hears your sincere questions and will seek to answer you in songs on the radio, messages on road signs, or conversations with friends. Just ask.

⌒ DO THIS ⌒

Raise your hand, speak your truth, and question everything. Get curious. Let yourself wonder and wander outside the box. Ask often, "What is the purpose?" and be willing to wait for the answer. Become committed to learning more.

Chapter 10

Stretch and Strategize

———

There is nothing my holiness cannot do.
—A Course in Miracles

Back in LA, August was hot and Miss Universe was hotter. She was back with a low-cut vengeance. Maybe she never left. She would help carry in the overnight bags when Reed would deliver a sleeping Owen after a long day of fun at the rich lady's house. I watched her eyes scan our shabby chic bungalow, which was heavy on the shabby and lean on the chic. I could not help taking in her polished perfection against our low-budget backdrop. It was mind-boggling how strategically sexy she was, how put together and on point. And speaking of points, hers were pushed up, present, and accounted for. She had a well-studied Victoria's Secret way of displaying her beautiful boobs.

It was nothing short of mesmerizing. Then she would ceremoniously grab Reed's arm so he could help her navigate the stairs in her stilettos. I could not help but feel that it was all for show; this was a woman groomed in stilt walking, saucy struts, and fancy pivots. If I could not appreciate her choice in men, I could at least admire her showmanship.

To try and escape the heat and the small confines of our tiny home, Owen and I would spend more time at the beach. The entertainment industry goes dead in the summer months, but I had a few commercials running and was still doing good business with the kids' parties.

With my free time, I began having parties and gatherings at my house. I found myself hosting baby showers and get togethers and every day, run of the mill Tuesday night parties. Bottom line, I was drinking more. If there was a reason to get everyone together, I was the catalyst. I knew this was a great escape and a grand distraction. Skye would often raise her brow at the crazy parade of creative people that would fill the house with song and dance and merriment. But, oh, I loved a good party.

I was ragefully busting free from the confines of my old identity, the young housewife from Sunnyside, Queens, the lonely new mom of Beverly Hills adjacent, the failing wife of Reed. I was done being pushed by pain and now I was being pulled by a vision. It was just that my vision was a little tipsy. I was over the rough patch and just wanted to have a little fun.

My parties would leak into the early hours of morning with cameo visits from celebrity guests. When all was said and done, I would find myself hung over and strung out for days.

Along with the alcohol, I began to quench my thirst on positive thinking, mysticism, and philosophy. I was attending Saint Monica's Church, going to yoga, and devouring books like

Julia Cameron's *The Artist's Way*, *The Alchemist* by Paulo Coelho, and *Women Who Run with the Wolves* by Clarissa Pinkola Estés. I also gulped down anything I could get my hands on by Louise Hay and dove deep into Paramahansa Yogananda, especially his book, *Let There Be Light.* These teachers tilled the soil of my soul, and my soil definitely needed some tilling.

Then of course there was Skye, with her illuminating wisdom. She would roam through the house in her silk kimono, dropping gems like a drunken jewel thief. "Pretty, you need to cut out all the barnacles."

"Sorry? Did you say cut the barnacles?"

"Yes, all the extra fat, the static."

"Like what?" I asked, growing impatient with her poetic ways.

"The parade of takers that you entertain, what do you get from that?"

"It's fun?"

"It has to be more than fun."

"Really? What's more than fun?"

"Having a life that pops."

"Okay."

"You are mindlessly picking up relationships like a garbage collector, and I just want to know what you are getting from it."

"They are my friends," I defended. "Isn't that good enough?"

"Depends. Do you want to have a good enough life?"

"No, but do I really have a choice?"

She waved her copy of *Unlimited Power* by Tony Robbins. "You got to set yourself up to win, set some goals, take some actions, get yourself a life that sizzles and pops."

I was aiming at survival mode . . . sizzle and pop was reserved for bacon. But I didn't mention that to her because she was on fire with one of her early hour sermons.

"If you want sizzle, you do the melting prayer."

"Melting prayer?" I asked.

"Yes, it's good to use for losing weight and clearing confusion. 'God, melt from me all that does not serve.'"

"Okay," I said, not really sure if she was just spitting this out as it came to her or if this was an actual thing.

"Then you gotta stretch."

"Like yoga?" I asked.

"Mental stretching," she corrected without interrupting her train of thought. "If you are not stretching, you are shrinking. When was the last time you really asked yourself to stretch out, past your comfort zone, new territory?"

"Well moving here," I answered in a mildly defeated way.

"No, that was not a choice; you were subject to someone else's decision. When was the last time you really stretched?" She didn't stop for my answer. "If you are not stretching, you are just regurgitating that same old thing. You are just filling the seats without any criteria."

Her mad ramble hurt my brain a little. Not only was she right, but I actually didn't see it as a problem. I rested a great deal in fate. If you were under my nose, and if you wanted to be my friend, then great. Fill the seat, jump in the van, and let's get rolling. It's good enough. I guess I was living a "good enough life."

"You need to get clear and look into every area of your life and imagine the optimal idea. You have to be the visionary for your own life. And another thing," she said, while rubbing my moisturizer into her hands, "just because you put a wall up when it comes to romance does not mean you actually changed anything. When your sabbatical is over, you are going to attract the same old thing, unless you begin asking bigger questions, getting clear, and setting goals."

"Like what?" I asked, feeling defensive and intrigued at the same time.

She leaned back like she was a magician ready to pull a rabbit from a hat. "Well, what do you want?" I stared back at her, unsure where to start. "You could have the guy of your dreams, but first you gotta know what he looks like, what he smells like, what he sounds like, and where he lives."

"Seriously?" I asked. "Sounds like stalking."

"The guy of your dreams could be knocking on your door, but if you don't know what you want, you might mistake him for the mailman." She turned abruptly and stepped out onto the porch to stretch in the sun.

"What if the guy of my dreams *is* a mailman?" I asked, trying to be witty.

"Well, you let him in and check out his package." She winked and bowed and then went from plank to cobra with the ease of the wind. "If you want a different outcome, you gotta draw a different map. Stretch and strategies!" She said, smiling, and then she lifted her ass and moved into downward dog.

That night I got out a journal and began to write. It was like taking dictation from my heart. Just like I had done a few months prior with my job situation. If I could pick the man of my dreams, what would he be like? I heard Skye's voice in my ear, "Don't fill the seats, just get clear on your desires. What do you want?"

I wrote a list of characteristics first: funny, kind, supportive, easy to be around, handsome. Then I began to stretch. I imagined what he looked like, what he smelled like, what he sounded like, and where he lived. Of course, these bits of information made me aware of things I had never thought of before, like the fact that I wanted a man to smell like cedar chips and tobacco. Who knew? That I wanted a man with sincere eyes that were as deep and blue as the sea. It was a fun exercise, so I kept going and began to write out all my dreams, one at a time and in detail.

After I was done with that, I wrote about my car and my career and my home and my bank account and health and all the nooks and crannies of my life. I began to imagine what it would look if I were to stretch. I started to realize that it was not just about how things looked, but how I felt about them.

I took this time to think about everything, and I began paying closer attention to the energy. I would check in on everything. If it did not feel right, it most likely was not ideal. I began trusting the energy and trusting myself. If I felt light and free, then I would move forward. If I felt spastic and sticky and needy, I would lean back. I made no apologies for the direction that my awareness led me

I started asking bigger questions like, "Do I love this so much that I would do it on a cold, dark, street corner with no one watching?" I loved recognizing that I had the power to choose differently. Skye was right. After all, I was dealing with a clean slate, so I wanted to be sure that I did not fill it with the same old stuff. I was done being wishy-washy and watered down, I wanted to be a hot knife through butter.

It was not easy unrooting all this old programming, but I knew that a life laced with lies and unsound loyalties would leave me feeling unfocused, confused, stagnant, fractured, and stuck. So, I began to question everything. It did not really change things right away to be honest; in fact, the truth is that some things got pretty bad before they got better.

I began to do the melting prayer, asking the Divine to melt from me everything that was not serving, everything that was keeping me stuck or frozen.

Turns out, there was a lot of pain stuck in my frozen places. And a lot of benefit to keeping things buried. But healing happens in the light, and I was ready to look at a few personal abandonments that I had tucked away. Drawing a new map would mean surrendering the old one. At times, I felt like I was walking in the dark and some miles were rockier than others.

After a particular rough couple of days, I had what I might call a little meltdown. The good news was that the melting prayer was working. I was up for a TV series that I did not get. I had just finished working a really long Pocahontas party out in the sun without sunscreen, so I had a horrible sunburn up my right arm, and of course because of the odd neckline I had a weird sunburn line. Reed was late picking up Owen, and the brakes on my car were freaking out. I felt agitated and resentful and overwhelmed. I was sitting on our back porch with my head in my hands, ruminating once again on how hideous Reed ended up being and wondering if this race I was running would ever end or get easier.

Skye joined me on the porch and handed me a glass of sweet tea. It was the smallest act of kindness, but at the time, I felt so depleted that it just broke me open. My Pocahontas make-up went dripping down my face, and I couldn't even find the words to explain how busted I felt at the moment. She just sat there, handing me tissues.

"Empty it all," she said gently.

I never had someone actually encourage me to cry it out. I was raised on "suck it up" not "empty it out."

"I wrote down all the things that I had hoped for, but what the hell difference does it make? Now I only see how far I am from the life of my dreams, and nothing I am doing seems to be working."

"'What you seek is seeking you.'"

I looked up at her. "Are you quoting fortune cookies?"

She rolled her eyes. "That's Rumi. This is normal. It's a labor pain, you just got to breathe through it, you got this."

"Reed is such an asshole."

She stayed quiet. "Hey, you want a total game changer?" she finally asked like a street corner drug dealer. I looked up at her, sincerely at the end of my rope. She continued. "You have to start praying for Reed. For his highest good."

"What? Wait, what? Pray for whom? For what?" I shook my head. "That can't be right."

She looked out at the yard and repeated her line while taking in the sunset as if she was in some Tennessee Williams play. I almost detected a slight drawl in her tone. But that could have been my imagination.

"You just have to do it. Do you want peace of mind or not?" In the midst of this broken moment, I had no choice but to trust her. She hadn't been too far off so far.

"'Out beyond ideas of wrongdoing and rightdoing, there is a field. I'll meet you there.'" She whispered like a prayer, and then turned to me. "That's Rumi too and also that's possible."

"If you say so."

When I first started praying for Reed, I was not really sure what to say. "God, bring Reed his highest good," and then I would do an Our Father, or a Hail Mary. Then I stumbled upon the book,"The Prayer of Jabez."

Oh, that you would bless me and enlarge my territory! Let your hand be with me and keep me from harm, so that I will be free from pain.

I read about how powerful it was, and since it was short and sweet I figured I would give it a try.

I would wake every morning and say it three times for Reed and three times for myself. Throughout the day, I would say it whenever resentment came up. So basically, there was not too much time when I was not saying it. It is not easy to pray for your former husband. It is challenging to ask that God's hand be with your perceived enemy, but really, whose hand would be better? I also found it difficult to pray to have Reed's territory expanded, and yet I knew that if I were not willing to give that to him, I would only be preventing myself from enjoying it too.

It began working right away. I could feel the toxicity that I felt when I thought of him begin to dissolve, and I was paying more attention to the things that I wanted to stretch into.

Then November came; I was eleven months into my twelve-month sabbatical, and I got an interesting phone message. It was Will from theater group, so-cute-he-makes-you-gasp Will. He wanted to talk with me about a project he was working on.

"I'm doing some research for a piece I'm writing about single mothers. Could I come by and ask you a few questions?" I had a funny feeling about his request. I couldn't possibly be the only single mom that he knew. I smelled something funny, like cedar chips and tobacco. I called him back and invited him for dinner, so he would get to see what being a single mom was all about. That night, I wore a simple salmon-colored sundress, swept the floor, lit a candle, and made a single mom's kind of dinner—Dinty Moore Beef Stew over noodles. I didn't want him to think that I was some kind of Martha Stewart type. If I learned anything from all this time off, it was that it was best to show up and tell the truth.

He didn't actually eat dinner with us, it was really just Owen, but Will didn't make the mistake of asking if I rinsed the noodles. So, that was smart on his part. I put Owen to bed, and Will and I hung out in the living room on my couch. It all felt a bit odd and disorientating. Was this an interview? Was he going to ask me questions? I felt self-conscious.

"You want a beer?" I asked.

"Sure," he said, and I got up to grab one from the fridge all the while thinking, *Play it cool.* I could hear my sisters' voices in my head.

"You should hook up with Mr. Comments."

"My sister's thought you made great comments," I heard myself blurt out.

"What?" he asked, obviously oblivious to what I was referring to.

"No, I mean when my sisters came out to the theater group, and I did that dumb song, yeah, they just . . . they thought that you gave great feedback." I was totally busted and bad at the whole playing it cool thing.

"Well you're a great actress," he said with a smile, maybe a bit too amused at my bulky banter. "You put up good stuff so it's easy to . . . you know . . . you give me something to comment on."

"Thanks. Skye thought my first song was pretty shitty."

He looked for a moment, weighing he words and then said, "Yeah, well no, that. Yeah that song was pretty shitty."

We laughed.

"But you," he took a longer pause, "you were great." I just smiled.

"It's putting yourself up there and being so brave and this." He gestured to Owen's room. "All that you are doing. It's cool. It can't be easy and yet you keep . . . you're doing it."

"Yeah, I guess."

Aside from that, the topic of being a single mom never actually came up. Mostly, we talked about life and his recovery from cancer and the theater and being actors. I told him about the guy, Carl, and seeing him and the little cowboy hat and how he'd given me two strikes.

"Two strikes? You? How is that possible?" He asked incredulously.

I laughed. "It didn't matter, really, because I was not actually dating anyone for twelve months anyhow." I may have added that last part just to be transparent about where I was at.

And that's when he made his move.

"If you're going to date anyone, you should date me," he said in a casual yet earnest way.

I just laughed and moved a little further down the couch away from him. Oh lord, I was really not ready for this. Yes, I had come so far. I had found myself, my footing, my voice. I had begun to see how to navigate life on life's terms, and I was even learning how to deal with Reed. But my heart was still healing, and I was gun shy to say the least.

He thanked me for having him over and explained that he needed to get up early the next day for a modeling gig. He was hired to do a shoot for the Cosmo calendar.

"Well, aren't you fancy?" I said. "Mr. Cosmo!" I am not sure if it came off as snarky or sarcastic. I am not even sure how I had intended it to come off. I was literally a bundle of awkwardness and trepidation.

He didn't seem to take offense either way, just sort of laughed and grabbed his jacket. He thanked me for taking time to talk. I thanked him for his visit and walked him to the door. On his way out, he turned and stood on my front porch under the light looking back at me, and I knew in that moment that he had definitely not come to interview me for any writing project. I stood holding the door open while a slight evening wind ruffled my dress. He dug his hands deep into his red fleece jacket, thanked me again, and turned to go. It was all very gentle and easy, and yet felt very fragile, like walking on a frozen pond and wondering if it will really hold you this time.

I watched through the window as he made his way out through the side yard then out the gate, and I sat back down on the couch and tried to gather my thoughts. Before I got too far, Skye came through the door with a smile that hung like a droopy hammock from ear to ear.

"Was that Will just leaving here?" she asked with more enthusiasm than I had seen, well, ever.

"Yes, it was. He just came over to talk about a writing project he is working on," I replied, trying to sound normal and casual.

"At night?" she pressed.

"Well, yes," I shrugged.

"And you're wearing a dress, and you lit a candle?" she prodded.

"I . . . well, yes. I did that," I said, trying to figure out the rationalization behind why I had worn this dress and lit that candle. "I lit a candle, and I wore a dress," I stated flatly, in hopes of scraping any extra meaning off the facts.

"Okay," she smiled. "Good for you. I like it," she gushed as her eyebrows rose and her duck lips came back.

I stared defensively as she nodded meaningfully.

"No, it's not like that," I said, holding my hands up to push off the unwanted accusations. "It was just a conversation, and I am not . . . I still have seven weeks left and—"

Skye zeroed in on me, "Did he ask you on a date?"

"No," I replied like a nervous game show contestant trying to get the right response in the shortest time. "I mean, wait, yes, he did. I think he did. Well, he said that if I were going to go on a date with anyone, which I am not because I am not dating, then I should go on a date with him. But that's . . . that was not him asking me out on a date." I stared back at Skye completely confused. "Was it?"

She raised her hands to the ceiling and turned her body around in a spastic Robin Williams gyration kind of way. Then she stopped, composed herself, and took a deep breath. She placed both hands on her hips, looked at me knowingly, pointing one long, manicured figure toward the back gate where Will had just exited. "Maureen, that is your mailman. Do not get in your own way."

I swallowed hard, and my gut hit the floor. I felt like I was being asked to jump into an elaborate game of Double Dutch, with Skye and Mr. Cosmo swinging ropes at either end and me standing outside it all trying to figure out how to jump in without getting caught or screwing things up. Skye made her way into the kitchen and grabbed the pot of noodles off the stove. I watched her add a scoop of butter and a hefty shake of salt, all the while smiling back at me. I loved her for her happiness, and I hated her for her happiness. The whole prospect made me dizzy. I got up from the couch and made my way to my bedroom.

It was mid-November, I had seven weeks left—I could not fold now. Even if it was Will . . . Mr. Cosmo . . . my mailman. No matter who it was, I needed to finish strong.

I had made plans for Owen and me to head back to New Jersey for Thanksgiving. Two days before we were set to leave, Will called.

"Hey, I just wanted to say thanks again for the other night."

"Yeah, you're welcome. No problem."

"It was great talking. You're a good mom."

"Well, thank you. That's nice."

"It's not nice, it's just true. I wouldn't say you're a great cook, 'cause Owen looked like he was eating dog food."

I laughed. "Yep, dog food for kids. But he likes it so . . . How did the shoot go?"

"It was great. Do you want to have dinner with me?"

"Oh." Long pause. "I'm not really . . . not dating right now," I explained. "I just made a promise—a vow and I still have seven weeks to go."

"Yep, I heard."

"Yep."

"So, the answer is yes then?"

"No, nope. No, that is not the answer." We talked for another hour. It was easy and normal, and he was funny, and I liked the sound of his voice. By the time I got off the phone I thought, *Seven weeks is going to be a terribly long time.*

I had one of his modeling cards that I brought home with me, so I could show my sisters. Maggie and Barbara lit up when they saw it.

"Oh my God! Mr. Comments!" they screamed. "We knew it!" Everyone seemed to "know" something about this budding friendship. He called me again while I was on vacation, and again we just seemed to be able to talk easily with each other. The hours flew by. He did not let up with the invitation to dinner. But I was set in my ways, even if I did hear Skye in my head whispering, "Don't get in your own way."

When I got back to LA, I was scheduled to go to an awards banquet with my friends Mary Beth and Jim from the theater company, who had the world's cutest baby. Mary Beth, who also happened to be friends with Will, called the day before the event.

"Hey there, listen, Will is babysitting for us, so why don't you let him give you a ride?"

"A ride where?"

"A ride to my house."

"Why?"

"Because it'll save time and the parking is bad here and . . . Maureen, don't be such a weirdo."

"I don't need a ride. I have a car."

"It's not a date. He is giving you a ride to save gas. It's good for the environment."

"Since when were you concerned about the environment?"

"It's good for everyone. Plus, I am a big fan of the environment. I have a compost jar on my counter."

"Fine. For the environment, I'll let him pick me up."

On the way to their house, Will handed me a mixed tape of love songs that he had made for me. Complete with a picture of him on the dust jacket with a thought bubble that read "girl of my dreams," and "Sleepless in Santa Monica." I held the mixtape in my hands, knowing this was not going to make the next seven weeks any easier.

On our way home from the event that night, I showed the tape to Mary Beth and Jim, who were drunk on the romance of it all.

"Play it!" they cheered and pushed the cassette into the player.

With each song, they acted like radio DJ's. "This one is going out to Maureen, with love from Sleepless in Santa Monica."

They attempted to read deeper meaning into it all. It was nice to feel courted and wooed. I had never been given a mixed tape before. I'm pretty sure that was the reason I caved and agreed to go on a date with him.

After all, when the train that you thought you missed suddenly shows up with an empty seat, you get the fuck on. Eleven and a half months was long enough. I mean come on, the guy made me a mixed tape!

And as simple as that, I was drawn back into the water. It felt like being a kid at the Jersey Shore when I would get knocked over by the waves and find myself twisted and shaken, sucking up sand, and swear I would never go back. And yet, the ocean was so damn beautiful it's hard to keep a safe distance and negate all the wonderful hours of riding the waves. It's easy to see why so many of us find our toes at the water's edge and our feet walking in.

Like moths to a flame we go. Because, in the end, the mesmerizing adventure is far better than sitting on the sidelines licking our wounds. We can make all kinds of promises, but as long as the world is peopled with persistent boys with the courage to share mixtapes or the technological equivalent, we romantic creatures will take the risk that life requires us to take for love.

Friday November 17th, I stepped out on my first date in almost a year. I was giddy and awkward. We went to a French place called Renee's. We ordered soup and drank wine and shared appetizers. I tripped when getting up to go to the bathroom and laughed way too loud and it was all lovely.

⁓ TOOL ⁓

Stretch and Strategize

We are each made for infinite possibilities. But we are the ones who need to stretch past the comfort zone, aim higher and dream bigger. As we set our sights and pray for our highest good and the highest good of all, we will see miracles.

Abundance or scarcity comes down to a projection issue. It is done unto you as you believe. This is a Universal law that cannot be broken. This is the law by which you create and were created. This is the law of love.

Love expands and extends, fear withholds and hordes. Fear sings a song of deprivation. "This is not enough, you are not enough, it will never work." These are the lullabyes that will rock you to sleep to your power. You have the ability to produce abundance or scarcity, depending on how you direct your energy. You get to choose love, joy, gratitude or fear, judgment, and unforgiveness.

⁓ DO THIS ⁓

Cultivate joyful expectancy, write down your deepest desires. If money were of no issue and you knew you could not fail, what would your perfect day look like? Where would you live, with whom, and what would you be doing? If you don't ask the bigger questions you will end up living a life of conformity instead of a life of creativity.

Spend one day using the melting prayer, "The Prayer of Jabez", or any prayer that is positive and personal. Do your best to stay close to it throughout the day. Plug it into your phone, post it to your mirror, and say it anytime that you feel anger or resentment. If you like how you feel at the end of the day, keep going.

Chapter 11

The Art Of Savoring

Love is the way I walk in gratitude.
—*A Course in Miracles*

After the first date, we picked Owen up from Laura and Dora's house. They came to the door and beamed at Will as if he were made of gold. He spoke Spanish to Dora as Laura and I whispered like school girls in the back room, while pretending to help Owen get his shoes on. Laura smiled and nodded her head, "He seems like a good one." I took a deep breath and exhaled.

On our second date, we went to La Cabaña, a great little Mexican restaurant in Venice. I ordered a bowl of tortilla soup. It was this bowl of soup that helped me to understand enlightenment. It was over this bowl of soup with warmth and spice and zest, sitting across from this man who had eyes that were so deep blue like the sea that I began to believe in sea monkeys again. It made no sense whatsoever but still I believed.

It was also over that bowl of soup that Will confessed to falling in love with me. As I said, I was enjoying the soup and he was enjoying me enjoying it. I am a verbal eater, especially when the food is good and I am hungry. But I was particularly noisy on this night.

He leaned in from across that table.

"You know, this feels kind of like that scene from *When Harry Met Sally*. But with Mexican people staring at us."

Unlike Sally, I was not faking it. I am telling you it was damn good soup. When I wiped the bowl with a chunk of bread, Will's face was bright red.

"What's up?" I asked.

"Nothing, it's just that I'm pretty sure I heard someone say, '*Yo quiero lo que tiene la gringa.*'"

"What does that mean?" I asked.

"I'll have what the gringa's having."

After getting an earful of how grateful I was for a little chicken broth, it got him thinking about other things that could make a good woman moan, and that was when he decided that our next date, at least by its conclusion, would not involve clothing. And, as it turned out, it didn't.

After the date after the "soup date" there was the next date, and the next, and the whole thing scared the hell out of me. Yet, as it turned out, there was nothing to be afraid of. Will was a good guy with a great sense of humor, kind and compassionate. In fact, he was just about everything I had listed, and truth be told, I had no idea how to deal with it. It all felt too good to be true.

Will had just been through his own personal earthquake. He was about eleven months in remission from stage three cancer. It was a terribly traumatic thing to go through at such a young age, but he was in recovery and things were looking up. He seemed to be doing great; his hair had all grown back. He was pretty much back to normal, except for one major thing: he was sterile. His doctor had warned him that this was a possibility and had instructed him to go to the sperm bank and put some fish on ice. As it turned out, it was a good thing that he took their direction because after he was done with chemo he was left completely sterile, no sperm, nothing. So, we took advantage of that. A lot.

⌐ TOOL ⌐

Savor

There is nothing sexier than a grateful being. They are the most attractive people on the planet. We love to stop and savor the sunsets, the chocolate, the scent of flowers. But what would it look like if you allowed yourself to take the time to take in everything in the most gracious and generous way.

Have you really taken in your friend's face, the commute to your job, your messy desk? When we allow ourselves to drop into the moment, we always come up with a new appreciation.

⌐ DO THIS ⌐

Become a master of savoring. Notice how you bathe, put on lotion, dress yourself. Allow yourself to go at the pace of peace and sip this second in slowly. Notice its noise and nuances. We tend to lose touch with our own enjoyment in the business of modern life. "We will cherish the high points," we tell ourselves. But that leaves many un-appreciated hours that can and will breed discontent. Discontent is a bad neighborhood where all your worst habits live. So order the soup. Just trust me on this one, and then savor the fuck out of it.

Chapter 12

Embrace Your Fire

——

T wo weeks into December, Owen and I gathered a wish list from Hollygrove Orphanage. It was something that we did every year. I would get the list for the kids that were housed there, each asking for one gift. Then I would get friends and neighbors and other actors to pick one, and shop for the gift.

Owen and I would gather up the toys, and on Christmas Eve we would dress as elves and deliver the gifts. It was a fun little tradition that made us happy to be part of the holiday magic.

We had gathered all the gifts and piled them under our Charlie Brown Christmas tree temporarily until it was time to deliver them. I had spent that day running around on auditions then rushed back to my house to meet up with Reed, who was dropping off Owen. When I walked in the door of our little love shack, it felt like a crew of feral cats had just escaped.

The room was in complete disarray and the gifts under the tree had all been torn open. It took me a while to realize that we had been robbed. I called the police, and then I called Will who happened to be on a soap audition.

The police came and took a report, the only things taken were Skye's old video camera and Owen's piggy bank. Not because there was not enough time to rummage through everything, but because those were the only items we had of value. The joke was on the Grinch who tried to steal Christmas. They had taken a screwdriver and slit open all the gifts, but when they saw that the gifts were all cheap kids' toys, they left them there.

When Reed showed up with Owen, I sent him to his room to play video games as I attempted to tape the packages back together. Reed stood in my living room helping gather up the discarded wrapping paper.

And then Will arrived. He came straight from his soap audition, which was to play the role of a heartthrob. He came right in through the kitchen and into the living room wearing jeans, a vest, and a cowboy hat. No shirt.

You know that moment that happens in all soap operas, right before the commercial when something major goes down? Like when the new boyfriend shows up without a shirt on just when the old husband happens to be visiting, and there is a soap opera standoff where they all give each other intense and meaningful looks? Well that is pretty much how it played out in my living room that day.

Reed looked at Will and then at me; I looked at Will and then at Reed; Will looked at me and then at Reed, and silence hung in the air. Then Will kind of pointed at the gifts, and the wrapping paper, and the tape, and then at me, and said, "Are you okay?"

I just nodded, one, because I was shocked at the absurdity of the moment; two, because I was still getting used to how insanely handsome Will was; and three, I had a bad feeling about how this was gonna go down.

To my surprise, Will nodded, reached his hand out to Reed and introduced himself, and turned back to me and said, "Okay, I am glad you're okay. I'm heading back to my place. I'll call you later."

And out the door he went like a devastatingly gorgeous apparition of Christmas future. Reed and I just stared at each other as I heard the door click and Will's car pull away.

Then the storm hit.

"You lied to me!" he seethed

"What?" I replied

"You said you were not dating for a year! You are a liar!"

"Are you serious?" I asked, completely shocked by his response. I was not really sure what to expect, but his calling *me* a liar was not even in my top one hundred guesses.

After the whole affair, the breaking of vows and trust and hearts, never in the past year had I called him anything even close to a liar. Though he deserved that title and more.

"What do you even care?" I shot back. "You're with Miss Universe!"

"You are a liar! I cannot believe that you would do this to me, to us. How could you?"

I watched him pace the little room like a shark in a fish tank. This little box of a room filled with a lopsided Christmas tree and damaged holiday gifts for orphans and yet the saddest thing of all was watching him pace. He was wrestling with the thought that I had already accepted. That this man who I had once loved with every thread of my being would now forever live in my rearview mirror. I felt his pain drip from his body and fill the room with sadness. I wanted to tell him that I was sorry, but I knew that I had no reason to apologize.

"You are a complete liar," he screamed one last time before heading out the back door, jumping in his car, and peeling away.

After all that we had been through in the last year, that was the real moment that I knew our relationship was over. Not because Reed had seen that I had moved on, but because I had seen that Reed lived in a universe of his own illusions. There was no way that I would ever understand the riddles and workings of his warped thinking, nor did I want to.

It was a day of break-ins, breakdowns, and a breakthrough. My ties to Reed were cut, and I was free in a way that I did not know would ever be possible.

For New Year's, Will and I spent the weekend in wine country, sampling ourselves into a stupor and filling the trunk of his Mazda with wine bottles. Will made me laugh, long and hard and constantly. I had always been a great audience, but his humor sat well with my heart. We began to spend every day together. And as funny as he was, he was not a clown. He was a man and began showing up like that in our lives.

One day, he came to our little love shack for dinner. I had given Owen a bath, wrapped him in some towels, put him under Skye's hairdresser chair in the corner, and turned it on. It was a fun way to get warm and cozy after the tub, and it gave me time to get dinner ready.

Will entered the house, took one look at Owen swaddled in a pink towel in a beauty salon chair, and told me, "That kid needs a little more male influence in his life. He looks like he is literally living in a vagina."

So, he made sure that happened. He was only twenty-seven, but he understood and welcomed the idea that a relationship with me meant a relationship with Owen. He did not shy away from either. He was the one to enroll Owen in soccer and then take on the role of team coach. He made Owen's lunches, drove him to school, and stepped in as a masculine presence in his life.

Will had a great little bachelor pad a few blocks from the beach. On the weekends, we would tuck Owen into his loft bed and then we would hang out, watch *Beavis and Butthead* and order Chinese food. It was not fancy or highbrow, but it was happy. Often, we would hear Owen's laughter as he hung his head over the loft and watched along with us.

Once a week we would go to Saint Monica's. Owen had been going to kindergarten there, and Laura still worked in the kids' care. Although I didn't know a ton of people in the parish, everyone seemed nice, and the priest usually delivered a motivating message.

One Sunday, we got dressed for church and I had the happy feeling that a certain degree of normalcy was returning to my life. We entered the church, made our way up the aisle, and found a place to sit down. For whatever reason, Owen did not want to go with the kids, so he sat between us on the pew.

The light shined through the stained glass and the scent of incense filled the sanctuary as the priest began to speak about marriage. It was some special day to celebrate those who had taken the vow of marriage with each other and he was going on about how sacred it was. Then he asked all the married couples to stand.

Because Will and I were not married yet, we stayed seated and tried not to look to conspicuous. But there we were in a sea of married couples with Owen between us, and the whole congregation staring at us like we were heathen sinners. Or at least that's what it felt like.

The priest continued babbling on about the idea that marriage was sacred and needed to be honored, and then he said the words that broke me right in half.

"Anyone who divorces his wife and marries another woman commits adultery, and the man who marries a divorced woman commits adultery and makes of her a harlot."

It was like a happy record had been ripped from the player.

"What did he just say? I am an adulteress? A harlot?"

I sat in shock while an ancient sadness filled every cell of my being. I sat in the beauty of that morning and realized that I was an outcast, a sinner. In the eyes of my beloved church, I was a harlot, and before I could stop myself I started weeping. It came with hot tears and hiccups and shaking shoulders. Will looked over at me and placed a hand on my back. I understood in that moment why Mary was weeping and how her tears were warranted, and what a horrible feeling it is to be tossed away by someone you loved.

I left the church that day and I never went back. One of the hardest things anyone will ever have to do is leave their tribe. But if I had been gifted anything from my classroom with Reed it was that there is no benefit in figuring out a way to stay in a relationship that does not fully honor you.

I was not an adulteress or a harlot. I was a holy woman not defined by man or church. After the tears dried up, what came next was equally surprising. It was nothing short of a whole and holy fire. I was lit and livid, mad enough to burn the whole house down.

Will had never seen me like this. He leaned back in his chair at the kitchen table and let me rant and rage. After a long pause that I would come to know as his signature style, he said, "I think I know a place that you will like. It's called Agape."

So that was the break-in, the break up, and the breakdown that eventually lead to my breakthrough. As harsh as this experience was, it would be the event that led me to a freedom that I didn't even know was possible.

Sometimes when you get woken up from a dream, it can feel agitating and uncomfortable. But nevertheless, I was waking up and I could no longer tolerate a sedate spirituality.

— TOOL —

Pay attention to what rattles you. The world will shake you, not to break you, but to wake you. You can decided to be defined by your tribulations or your resurrection. Women who have smashed glass ceilings have not done so via easy street.

The shaking is an invitation to pay attention. When the flower is ready to burst from the seed, it does not go gently. There is agitation, and aggravation that assist the process. There is usually a spiritual tenderization that precedes our breakthroughs.

Don't be scared off by your own fire. There is a flock of Phoenixes that live in you that are ready to rise with the prize. So let yourself get fired up in your own passion.

Though it may temporarily consume you, it will also transform you. Or you will simply burn through what holds you back. The fire pushes through the resistance so that we can break through to a reserve energy. This is usually connected to the fire in the belly and allows you to witness your power and passion so that you can experience yourself firing on all cylinders.

— DO THIS —

Dare to sit curiously close to what enrages you. This is important or you would not be so triggered. Do not fear your own fire. Throw yourself in a little bit, get your passion up. Take a risk and go to where the map has not been charted for you and burn yourself a new path. If you have been burnt, make a vow that this branding stops with you. Let your passion inform your platform and your massacres inspire your message.

Take time with your Divine to contemplate what fires you up. Then put your back into it. Live your life so that when the sand leaves the hourglass, you can stand in conviction and say, "I spent it. I lived it, my way, to the best of my ability. I did not phone it in, I did not back down, I lived fired up in my own truth and passion and on the cusp of my fear and in the constant state of stepping forward.

Chapter 13

Your Legacy

———

To forgive is merely to remember only the loving thoughts
you gave in the past, and those that were given you.
—*A Course in Miracles*

gape was a spiritual community on Pico that was right
next to Owen's school. The founder and minister was
Reverend Bernard Beckwith. I watched him walk to the
stage with a tribe of women and men surrounding him. It was
like a cat visiting a queen. They moved in a majestic way that
spoke of ease and grace and power and I was in awe.

Before he spoke, there was music that made the room stand
and sway, and then a woman came to the pulpit to do a blessing
on the minister and the message and the members. She introduced herself as a practitioner. I had no idea what that was, but
I felt myself sit up and take note.

What is a spiritual practitioner? How did she get in there,
how did that happen, and how can I follow her? The blessing

was not something that she had memorized, it was flowing from her like a river of wisdom and light, and when she was done she gently whispered, "And so it is."

My unsedated soul sighed and whispered back, "Amen."

After that, Reverend Michael Bernard Beckwith came to the stage. His presence was beautiful and open and generous. He spoke in verse, he spoke of vision, he channeled a sermon that was tailor-made for every cell of my being. Every idea penetrated my heart and wrapped me in a message that left me feeling whole and serene and home.

Agape would become my new community and the catalyst for my next chapter, where I would marinate in new thought and meditation and move into becoming a licensed practitioner.

I was like a dry sponge to water, drinking in all the good stuff. Letting all this truth wash over me and smooth the rough parts and loosen the barnacles.

In May, Will took Owen and me to the Theatricum Botanicum, a magical outdoor Shakespearean Theatre near Topanga Canyon. The place was dancing with fairies and good vibes, the land held a poet's history and an artist's heart.

We spread out a blanket, laid out some food, and smiled at each other as Owen went on a wild search for fireflies.

God could not have painted a more perfect moment. The faint music from the cast in a pre-show practice; the warm ocean air carrying the complex scent of red dirt and ancient wildfires and eucalyptus leaves. Under a trillion stars and a million twinkle lights, Will asked me to marry him.

It was so sincere and simple. Just, "Will you marry me?" I am pretty sure it surprised him more than it surprised me. My heart leaped, his eyes smiled, and Owen ran up and told us about a frog or a bug or a puddle that he had discovered, while the question hung heavy in the air between us. I didn't say yes, and I didn't say no. I just pretended like I didn't hear him and changed the subject. So much for all of God's efforts. I could almost hear the angels groan. "Strike One!"

In July, Will invited Owen and me to Madeline Island to meet his parents. The moment my foot stepped on the soil of the scared place I knew something in a way that words cannot contain. It was a feeling of returning, of rerooting and restoration. After dinner, we hiked out to a point where you could take in a view of the massive nature of Lake Superior.

"My family has come to this island for generations. It's where my grandparents lived and had their ashes sprinkled. This is the place where I've come every year of my life," he said while wrapping his arms around me.

"My grandparents and now my parents have loved this island—coming up here, year after year, having kids, making campfires, swimming."

"It's beautiful," I said. Even though those words only scraped the surface.

"Do you want that?" he asked. I looked into his blue eyes. "'Cause I want that. I want that with you."

I smiled.

"So whata'ya say? You wanta get married?"

This time, he held me in his embrace and looked me directly in the eye. There was no wiggling free and no desire to escape and this time I said, "Yes."

Three months later, on September 30th, on another island off the coast of California, we said, "I do."

I wore a vintage suit and held a bouquet of wildflowers.

It was just the two of us and a woman named Fern Wallace, who was about a hundred years old. We got her out of retirement to bless our vows. She also acted as the witness and the photographer. All our pictures were from the nose up or the neck down, but we loved that they were perfect souvenirs of our secret day.

Will had never been married before, so we also decided to plan a traditional wedding the following June at the Jersey shore, mostly for his parents and my sisters. My sisters hated the idea of missing a wedding.

The day after we eloped, Will moved into the love shack. It was seamless timing. The week prior, Skye got an offer to write for a few publications back in New York, and she was ready to return to her roots in the Big Apple.

It was a very busy time. Will had finished writing a feature film based on his experience with cancer, titled *The Setting Son*, that was set to shoot at the end of April. The storyline was about a brother who must choose between Olympic dreams or being around for his brother battling cancer.

There was a ton of behind the scenes pre-production work that needed to happen. We were working with a great team of friends who made the process fun. But still there was a ton of work, Will was writing and workshoping the script, we were casting and securing locations, working with the wardrobe team, and Screen Actors Guild and it was all so new. We had a steep learning curve. Sometimes it felt like we had rolled a snowball downhill and it was turning into an avalanche.

Because of the theater company, we had a tribe of actors who Will basically wrote parts for. Will was set to play the lead, and I was cast as the career-driven girlfriend who does not want him to surrender his gold medal dreams. Turns out it does help to sleep with the writer. We nailed down most of the work and headed to Jersey so that Will could meet my parents and we could share the wedding plan news.

My sisters were thrilled by the engagement and stopped calling Will Mr. Comments and started calling him Uncle Eye Candy. There were plenty of parties where everyone wanted to meet Uncle Eye Candy. But we were only there for a week, and I was sick the whole time with terrible flu-like symptoms.

Still I really wanted to go wedding dress shopping with my sisters. This was something I did not do the first time; I had just borrowed a dress from my sister Erin. In the hopes that this would be my last time down the aisle, I wanted my own dress. So we headed out to bridal land, where I modeled a few dresses with my sisters surrounding me with oohs and ahhs. I found the most beautiful dress, they gave the seal of approval, and I purchased it in an optimistic size too small. I had put on a little holiday weight, but I had six months to get in Wedding Day shape before the big day.

And then I started throwing up . . . pretty much every hour . . . like an amateur on Saint Patrick's Day.

"Maureen, are you okay?" My sisters asked.

"I feel car sick," I moaned.

"Maybe you're pregnant," they teased.

"It's impossible," I said. "Remember, my husband is sterile from chemotherapy. He has zero sperm."

"Good on ya" they cheered and raised a glass of holiday libations to toast my good fortune.

When we got back to LA, my nausea continued, so I thought it might be wise for me to take one of those pregnancy tests, just for kicks.

Then I took another, and another, each one informing me of the same news. I was in fact pregnant. Pregnant? How the hell did that happen? How could I get pregnant with a sterile guy? We called the sperm bank. They suggested that Will come in and get tested. By the end of the day, they called to say that yes in fact there was a sperm. One sperm.

"But you can isolate it and inject it into your wife's egg," they suggested hopefully. "It's a new process, that has been very successful." Will stopped them.

"My wife is pregnant," he offered. I could hear their laughter through the line.

"Well, you only have one sperm, but it was a really good swimmer." I sat in shock. This was the most twisted of plot twists. I was planning a wedding. I was supposed to be in a movie. I just bought a wedding dress an optimistic size too small! The look on Will's face as he contemplated the idea that his health had returned to the point that his body was fully functioning again, and that he was going to be a father, was enough to get me past my shock and awe. By this time, I was getting used to God's funny plot twists.

With the new calculations, a June wedding would have me hobbling down the aisle at six months. I called my sisters for advice.

"Look, Maureen, don't freak. You just have to take the dress to a tailor, have them rip the zipper out and put in a lace up back so the dress will expand with you. Then you push the date up and order an extra-large bouquet."

Resourceful Jersey girls have a life hack for everything.

Will and I pushed the wedding up to early April, and I walked down the aisle with my extra-large bouquet. My sisters went from calling Will "Uncle Eye Candy" to calling him "The Sperminator."

Before returning to LA, we spent a week in New York as a honeymoon of sorts: me and Will and Owen and my new in-laws. Because it always nice to have your five year old and your in-laws along for your honeymoon.

The truth was we were so busy with planning the wedding, the new baby, and the pre-production for the movie that we didn't really put any thought into a honeymoon. So, I was grateful for my mother-in-law taking the lead.

In New York, we went to see a couple of shows and enjoyed some amazing restaurants. This was the side of the city that I did not experience when I lived there as an actress busting my butt to book work.

And, of course, we spent a few days with Skye. In New York, she was in her element and on fire. She came straight up from the lobby to our hotel room. We could hear her like a linguistic locomotive making her way down the hallway. She brought her boyfriend Steven along for our approval but never gave us the opportunity to judge him.

"He's a brilliant actor—you have got to see him on stage—and an amazing writer, pure genius. Oh, Steven do your gorilla!"

"No, Skye."

"Do the gorilla! For Owen! Owen do you want to see Uncle Steven do the gorilla?'

Owen nodded with wide eyes and Steven did a pretty great impersonation of a gorilla that made Owen and Skye fall over laughing. Will looked at me for an interpretation, and I just laughed and shrugged.

When Skye loved you, she did it completely and there was no honest way that any mere mortal could ever live up to her accolades. But we all enjoyed watching her praise.

She came bearing gifts for Owen, stories of the current city events, and suggestions for restaurants, all in an uninterrupted monologue that left us amazed and admiring. She was as riveting as ever, and seeing her face lit me up.

She still treated me like the younger sister. When I complained of feeling sick and having a headache, she flew into action. "First off rub this lavender oil on your wrist and Maureen, those shoes are a big no. No wonder you are in pain, you need a basic pair of street Keds, pronto." Down the block we went and into the first shoe shop and within an hour my headache was gone. She was magic.

When it was time to leave we hugged in the middle of the city sidewalk.

"I am so happy to see you so happy Skye."

She smiled back at me. "We all deserve to be happy." Then she kissed me on the check and left a lipstick tatoo of her signature shade of Chanel, "Pirate."

I watched after her as she made her way down the street disapeared into the crowd. Little did I know that it would be the last time I would see her. If I had known I would have chased after her and milked her of all the unshared untapped wisdom and advice that still lived in her bones. If I had know I am not sure I would have let her go.

When we got back to LA, we began production on *The Setting Son*. We were only a few days into shoot when I got the call on the set.

"Maureen? This is Bean, are you sitting down?"

"Bean? Am I sitting down? Why?" I stepped outside of the home we were shooting in.

"I just need you to sit down." Her voice was thin and urgent. My mind raced, and my eyes began to fill with tears before my butt hit the wooden steps. "It's Skye."

"What? Is she okay?" My voice was thin and cautious.

"Ahh no. I am so sorry to tell you this, Maureen. Skye is dead."

From my body swelled a moan unlike any I had ever uttered.

"Nooooo!" I heard myself scream. "No, no, no, no, no!" I kept repeating because my mind could not accept this news in any way.

Bean continued on with the details of Skye's sudden death. It was a virus that she contracted a day after we left New York. She was battling it, in and out of the hospital, and there was nothing they could do.

I hung up the phone and after leaving a respectable puddle of tears in the stoop, I sat still and stared out at the world, not sure how to move from that moment. I felt ransacked and ravaged, broken open and emptied out. "Empty it out," I heard her say, and I did. But this time there was no sweet tea, no clever banter. It was the silence of the moment that I found the most devastating and all the "never wills" that followed and floated by my mind. Never will I see her again. Never will she see my new baby. Never will I find a friend to fill her shoes. Never will I stop missing her.

She had filled my head with wisdom and my heart with courage, held open her door and made room from my threadbare heart. She opened my eyes to wonders and gave me just enough of a bitch slapping to help me find my strength. She had told me I was a good storyteller, and so I made a vow that day on those wooden steps that before I left this blue marble, that I would honor hers.

That September 1st was Labor Day, so I took it literally and went into labor.

We called the midwife.

"I will be right there, start walking."

"Walking. Really?"

"Yep, best thing to do." I pulled on my Keds and Will and I must have circled Santa Monica twice. We walked.

The sun set, the moon came up, and we walked. By 10 o'clock, the contractions really picked up and I made my way back to our love shack. I was ready to go. I walked down the hall to our bedroom, and my eye caught the framed poster that was hanging on the wall. It was a picture of Will with an Arabian horse that he had shot a few years before he had cancer. The caption read, "This stud's for you." I let out a laugh and my water broke. Before the day was done, I gave birth at home, to our daughter Billie Rose.

On the wall of our bedroom hung the Cosmo calendar with Will's face staring back at me. My sterile husband, the stud. I marked the 1st with Billie's birthday and the 30th with our one-year anniversary. He really was Mr. September.

Being dumped for Miss Universe could only be eclipsed by something as incredible as being picked back up by Mr. Cosmo. I know the word is a shorter version of the word Cosmopolitan, but when I looked up the word cosmo the definition reads, "relating to the world or the universe." This was this final sign that I needed to remind myself once and for all that there really is a Divine wisdom working on our behalf, and that She happens to have a great sense of humor.

⌒ TOOL ⌒

We live in the cycle of life. Things will come and go. But nothing real can be threatened. Things of this world have an expiration date on them, if it can die, it will die. The best we can do in these circumstances is to celebrate. Celebrate it as it comes and while you have it. Honor it when it arrives and honor it when it passes. In all the changes there are still four words that can make a rich man cry and a poor man laugh, "This too shall pass."

The love that once was, will always be even if it changes form. Nothing real ever dies and what is real is love. So love more and fear less, don't forget to laugh and expect miracles when you least expect them.

⌒ DO THIS ⌒

Think about the legacy you have had on your world. Are there people that you have unfinished business with? Consider writing them a letter. If you feel at peace with everything, write your eulogy. Write out your legacy. Take an inventory of all the good that would not have happened if you had not been born. This is an interesting exercise that will give you clarity on what you truly value.

One last bit of advice, treat each day and each encounter as if it is your last. Even if you attempt to live like this for one day, you will dip into a greater sense of peace and appreciation and you will find true happiness. And everyone deserves to be happy.

Chapter 14

Be Kind to The Universe

———

When you meet anyone, remember it is a holy encounter.
As you see him you will see yourself.
As you treat him you will treat yourself.
—*A Course in Miracles*

Just as this book began with an ending, the story ended with a new beginning. Not for me, but for Miss Universe. I might not have caught it if I wasn't careful, but of course I was . . . careful that is. I cannot take all the credit for the miracle. It took all the king's horses and then some to put me back together so that, by the time she called, I had been prepared. That was when the real miracle happened, when she called.

It was a few years after Billie was born. I lifted the phone to hear her announce herself, Miss Universe was calling me. Yes, Miss Universe, the one with the great tits. She sounded shaken and scared, and asked if Reed was having an affair, if I had seen him with another woman. Her voice was weary, and I could tell she was confused.

"Yes, I've seen him with another woman," I told her. It was the truth, and she deserved it. Then she asked me something that I will never forget. It was a question that was delivered in a weak little voice that made me want to reach through the phone and shake her tiara off.

"Is she pretty?" she asked.

It was a fragile and vulnerable moment, a crazy daytime talk show moment, and I knew that I could have what was mine, what I had dreamed of, what I had been hoping and praying for. I could have my sweet and sadistic revenge. *Yes,* I could tell her. *She is magnificent.* I could rattle her cage with the careful description of perfect breasts and flawless forms. Yet, oddly, this invitation was not even a little bit tempting. Instead, something startling happened. I leaned back and let love lead the way. I suddenly felt great compassion for her. I stood a moment in her stilettos and experienced her shattered heart and I would not wish that on anyone. Nor would I be the cause of it if I could help it. I would step off the treadmill of mindless meanness and try to offer love.

I took a breath and listened to that still, small voice within me. I wanted to give her the truth, and the truth was that this new woman was very pretty. But what good would that information do her? "Was she pretty?" It dawned on me that she was just asking the wrong question. She didn't really want to know if the new lady was pretty what she wanted to know was, "Will I be okay? Will I land on my feet? It's crazy how fear has us asking all the wrong questions. We stood at the cusp of a new conversation that I don't think was lost in either of us. From my lips came a bolder truth, one that was wrapped in compassion and care and a wisdom that understood how connected we all are.

"Who the hell cares if she is pretty?" I heard myself state. "You're Miss Universe! Do you hear me? You're Miss *fucking* Universe. There is no one in the whole universe who is better than you. You cannot be insecure!" I heard her sniffle and then laugh and then sigh. Then I sniffled and laughed and sighed.

"I'm afraid that he will leave me," she confessed. And I heard myself tell her something that I had learned the hard way.

"He might. But don't worry. This is not the end. It's just the beginning." This unplanned moment tasted so much better than all that revenge I had been cooking up all those years. As she hung up the phone, I knew that her journey was not going to be easy. She too would learn to get back up. And when one of us rises, we all rise.

— TOOL —

We are each members of humankind. Being kind is part of our branding. What comes around goes around so extending compassion to everyone, even and especially the ones that you don't want to be nice to is just smart. There is a law of cause and effect, that says "all you do will affect you." It is done unto you as you believe and as you treat others. The world that you invest in is the world you must live in. Or as I like to say, "there is no pissing section in the pool." Don't kid yourself, karma is a bitch that you do not want to mess with. Cultivating compassion in your life is an undervalued but priceless resource.

— DO THIS —

The golden rule is a thread that is woven in all religions. It makes good sense to treat others as you would like to be treated. Make a practice of seeing everyone as someone's daughter or son. Not only will this allow you to dismantle potential wars, but it will ensure that you retain all your precious energy of more positive creative endeavors.

Always strive to help her up no matter who "she" is. This is the only way we will ever see our share of equality. Women may have been burned at the stake, but we have been branding each other ever since. It's time to lay all that down and move in a true direction of peace and empowerment.

Chapter 15

Come Clean

───────

Love holds no grievances.
—A Course in Miracles

The journey that started with falling was just the beginning of my rise. And rise I did. I went on to have two more kids with Mr. "I'm sterile," and then like a good little bin diver I took a deep dive into the spiritual side. It was not all ease and grace. In fact, before I rose I hit one more bottom.

I had been circling the sober conversation since I was eighteen. I knew I had a severe addiction to alcohol. It had been my truth from my first experience with alcohol. I had been to the twelve-step meetings. But during my years of marriage to Reed and even the years after, I was so driven by the fear of failure, that I took great efforts in managing my drinking. Being sole support for Owen, I knew that if I went down, he would have to go with me. That was not something I could live with. Staying sober or at least mostly sober, was something that I did because

I knew in the back of my mind how fast I could slip if I were not careful.

But now with Will, co-parenting and co-partying, the game was on. Will could have a drink with dinner like a normal civil person. He would open a bottle of wine, like they do in the movies, two normal grown ups having an easy glass of wine. But for me, it was never normal or easy, one drink was too much, and two drinks were never enough. The nights would end in one of three ways, blacking out, passing out or vomiting.

It was easy to rationalize my drinking because I was not a guzzle down the whiskey kind of drinker and in most circles I would be described as a "high bottom." I had no DUIs, no rehab, no jail time, no homeless jags, never lost a job . . . that I was aware of. I was just a really thirsty girl, with an inability to stop. That was it. But that was enough to qualify me.

Alcohol was like another sister to me. She made me feel happy, and relaxed. She made me laugh and helped me to open up about myself. She made it easy to connect with others and at the same time she protected me from them. I used alcohol the same way I used acting, to help me disappear, to help me hide.

The real me was a little awkward, nervous and afraid of my own truth. Drunk me was everyone's best friend. Everyone loved "drunk me." She was better in every way, funnier, faster, wittier, in fact "drunk me" was even more psychic. Yep. My friends would call me "the psychic drunk." I am not sure if I became more psychic when I was drunk or if I just had no inhibitions about telling people exactly what I thought. Either way it was a fun party trick and I was all about having fun.

It was not in my deepest pain that I hit bottom, it was when things were happy. I think that is why it came as such a surprise.

It started out innocently enough, Will would open a bottle

of wine with dinner and by dessert I was tapping a keg. My motto has always been, "the more the merrier!"

Hosting parties was my own form of social activism. "I bring people together! I provide a service." I would declare whenever Will raised an eyebrow about my announcing another party that we were hosting. My addiction to alcohol was matched only by my addiction to showing people a good time.

The bigger the party the harder I'd fall. Mornings were met with thick confusion, searing pain and debilitating guilt, sometimes it would take a couple days to fully recover. When the album was finally ripped from the needle, it was hard to say goodbye to the hostess with the mostess. I liked my drunk self, a lot of people liked my drunk self. As a people pleaser I hated having to cut her off. But my life was beginning to suffer and I was in danger of losing something real, my relationship with Will.

I attempted quitting unsuccessfully many times and I left a long trail of broken promises. "This time it will be different." or "This time, I will drink like a normal person." or "This time, I won't drink tonight" or "I will just have one." or "I will drink only on the weekends." or, or, or . . . each one more futile than the next.

Hitting bottom was less dramatic and more of a slow and subtle slide. The list of things that I vowed that I would never do got shorter and shorter. I would never drink in the morning, I would never drink all night long, I would never show up to the set still drunk from the night before. But I ended up doing all the things that I had thought I would never do.

My drinking was having a negative consequence on my life. But I was a die hard optimistic, rosé colored glasses drunk who got more and more optimistic with each cocktail.

It was a slow and almost imperceptible fade to black, or black out as was the case. I had a strong tolerance for pain. I didn't hit bottom as much as I woke up to my own powerlessness and my inability to try and manage my disease. I had plenty of warning signs on the way down. I didn't stop even after morning after morning of waking in pain and shame trying to piece my nocturnal shenanigans together. I didn't stop when I began missing appointments and engaging in elaborate lying to cover my tracks. I didn't even stop when I showed up to set with blurry vision and beer breath. The thing that finally caused me to pause was when my drinking began to mess with my relationship with Will.

It was an especially scary Halloween at a theatre company party. We were invited to come dressed as a famous dead person. Our friend Tim was John Denver, Will was Freddie Mercury and I was dressed as JonBenet Ramsey, complete with the "Little Miss Boulder" sash. Don't judge me it was a contest. I wanted to win.

We headed out to the party, but as the evening was winding down, I was just getting started. Will was ready to leave. This was becoming our pattern, we would go out, Will would go home and I would help close the party down which actually meant keep it going. There were always actors who were up for a good time. That night I came dangerously close to doing to Will what Reed had done to me. It was not that our relationship was missing anything, it was simply that I was missing from our relationship. I was losing myself at the bottom of a bottle and bad things happen at the bottom of a bottles.

It was a Bridges of Madison County moment when I was given an invitation to make a night of it with this guy who I was friends with. We had been working on a play together and as you can imagine lines can get blurry. Add a little alcohol to that and you got yourself a wildfire. Crossing the line with him made sense and at the same time it made no sense at all. I was not living in the real world. I found my way to the bathroom, slid down the wall and realized that I was about to take myself on a trip that I could not return from. I tucked my chin to my chest and whispered a sincere and desperate prayer.

"Dear God, please help me not ruin my life. I will do whatever it takes to not fuck up my life. I do not want to go down this path, I do not want the pain that will come with it." At this point I knew the wreckage that was waiting if I should toss out what was real and right for what was right now. Somehow I got up, got myself home and dodged that bullet.

The next morning I called my one sober friend Kimi. She had been an award winning soap actress who had a quick rise and a harsh fall, but she also had a great head on her shoulders. I thought she was an anomaly the way she could hang out, stay sober and still have fun.

"I think I need to go to one of those meetings," I told her.

"No problem, let's meet for coffee and then we can head to my home group," she said through the phone.

The next evening over coffee I confessed my reckless ways with alcohol and how I realized that I had no idea how to stop.

"You are in the right place," she smiled. "This is not an ending, this is the beginning of your miracles." Little did we know how right she was about that.

"I could be up for that," I said, even though I had no idea how this sober gig was even possible.

"At the meeting they're going to invite you to stand and identify yourself as an alcoholic. You don't have to, but it works way better if you do."

We drove to the meeting in the Valley. This time I was ready, this time I was willing. This time when they asked for newcomers, I raised my hand.

"Please stand," said a voice from across the room. It was surreal. The room was both bright and blurry and I was shaking in my boots, but I stood.

"Would you like to introduce yourself?" the voice said. I look down at Kimi. She nodded and mouthed the words, "Just say it," like an encouraging stage mom, feeding me my line from off stage. I looked back out at the room and opened my mouth, but nothing came out. Just air and a few squeaks, but my voice was gone. Suddenly the room began to morph and twist like a Fellini film. All the warped faces looking back at me all whispering, "just say it." The longer I stood, the louder they got. Till someone yelled from across the room, "Just say it!" and with all the courage and strength that I could muster I pushed the words out. They were barely a whisper, they came with tears, but they were delivered. "I am Maureen and I am an alcoholic." No sooner had my words hit the air that the room lit up in approval and replied, "Welcome Maureen" and I sat back down.

I had no idea what was in store or even how someone would or could actually stay sober. But I had nowhere else to go, so I would leave my tipsy tribe and venture into territory my people had no map for. Sobriety.

How was I going to tell my family and friends? Drinking was a huge part of my identity. I was the psychic drunk for God sakes. They say in AA that sometimes God will do for you what you can not do for yourself. I was a couple weeks sober and feeling like crap, but I just kept working a program, going to meetings and putting one foot in front of the other. There were events on the horizon that I could not imagine navigating sober. New Year's, family holidays, weddings, funerals, St. Patrick's day . . . I honestly wondered, do those events even happen for sober people?

At twenty days sober I started getting sick. Like physically ill.

"You're just detoxing," Kimi suggested when I showed up at our morning meeting nauseous and green. "This will pass, I promise."

It didn't pass, it lingered till day 25 and on day 30 I was still feeling lousy. Around this time I realized I had skipped my period. Humm isn't that interesting. Not that pregnancy was an option. I was on the pill and my husband was basically sterile except for that one sperm which I had already caught. Still I thought I should at least rule that out before going to the doctor.

On my 30th day sober I stood up to get a 30-day chip and promptly excused myself to go pee on a stick in the bathroom. I stared down at the little blue plus sign and realized that I was also about 30 days pregnant.

Until that moment I had no idea if I could actually stay sober for myself, but I knew I could and would stay sober for this new baby.

When I shared the pregnancy news with Will he was thrilled and shocked.

"I think we need to start looking to move to a bigger place."

"What? No, we love our home, our little love shack."

"Yeah, but we'll have to get velcro suits for the kids and stick them to the walls to sleep."

I looked around our home; this little shack had been a safe chrysalis for so much healing and yet I knew Will was right, it was time to fly.

We would start to look for a home in Studio City. It was time to pack up and give away anything that would not be making the move with us.

There were many trips to the Goodwill. Between the letting go of stuff, being sober, and my pregnant hormones urging me to nest, I felt like I was shedding faster than a Siberian Husky on a summer day.

Under my bed were years of journals, notebooks, and old scripts that I had written or read for. I went through each one like a meticulous inventory. Reading all my mad rambles, all the beliefs and ideas that had gotten me to that moment, I was surprised by how much fear and pain lived on the pages. After I was done reading them all, I lit the fire pit and I burned them.

Every last one went in. It took me a full day. But I was determined to leave the old story behind.

It was a modern day fire ritual and I imagined all the energy being freed. Like the Phoenix rises from the ashes liberated from the weight of the world.

I had held onto so much that was not mine, so much that did not serve me. Like keeping rotting food in the refrigerator. I wanted it gone. I wanted to be vigilant about clearing it all.

I thought of it like a farmer burning the old crops, to clear space for new growth. I wanted to be sure that I only planted what I actually desired. I didn't want to make my past wrong; I just wanted to let it go.

Burning the dead was a common practice among ancient cultures. When a soldier died in battle the bodies, too heavy to carry home, would be burned and the ashes delivered. Cremation was considered a hero's death. These old journals and stories were my dead soldiers. I was grateful for their service as I placed each one into the fire.

Although these old stories had defined me I could not let them deny me. So I burnt the stories of death and divorce and denial about addictions, I cremated it all down to ashes.

As I sat feeding the fire I heard my Divine say, "Feed your desires and starve your distractions. Do not watch the embers that will only make you feel nostalgic and morose. Instead raise your eyes to the smoke and watch the energy that was once trapped in these stagnant places and old scripts, watch it all be freed, liberated and be glad."

I lifted my eyes and as the smoke rolled over me I sent out a silent prayer, "With the liberation of this smoke I too am liberated from all my past stories that no longer serve my highest good." The fire sang in pops and sizzles as the moon began to rise. I continued long after the serenading cicadas went silent. And just when I got to the last of what could be burned I witnessed the most beautiful thing. It was an old scrap of a newspaper clipping that went floating above the fire and as it did it twisted and turned and twirled in what felt like a holy dance designed just for me.

I was mesmerized by the message of the moment delivered by this old piece of throw-away scrap paper. I was watching this old trash be transformed and lifted. Like the ashes of the love letter from long ago that rose and fell on my counter top. I was on the other side of the story now, as I took it all in I felt a sincere appreciation for this old newspaper boldly living its second life as a dancer. Where once it was seen only as a page of expired current events, sent to deliver bad news to bored people, now it was a dancer. At the hour of its demise is when, it looked to all the world that it was done and doomed, a secret second breath of life rushed in to lift it. Twirling and swirling for this grateful audience of one.

What else is possible I thought. What else still lives on in my bones?

In the next weeks we began looking at homes in Studio City. Within a month we were moving into our new home. Sitting sideways on the toilet was in the rearview mirror. The new home had a pool and palm trees and celebrity neighbors.

The first week in the new place I got invited to a mom's group. It was the mom mafia of Studio City. These were high power executive moms who scared the shit out of me. They had a life hack and a best practice for everything. They took motherhood seriously. It was an Olympic sport that could and should be mastered and won. Planned and measured, I let them know that for me motherhood had come because I was sloppy and fertile and happened to be married to the sperminator. They let me stay anyhow, tucking me and my messy ways under their wings. They taught me what it meant to really pay attention to the details and the art of taking radical care.

It was a magical time filled with signs, symbols and synchronicities. During my first year of sobriety, Will and I went back up to visit Madeline Island. We were driving to the airport to catch a plane back to LA, when I asked Will to pull over, so we could check out an old bookshop. As I have mentioned, I'm a terrible packer, and my suitcase was already stuffed to the gills. I had no business shopping for anything, but that didn't stop me. I had pirate blood and like a good bin diver I was always on the look out for buried treasure.

As we entered the shop, the bell on the door announced our arrival, and an old cat lifted his head to welcome us. My curiosity kicked in and I optimistically tried to juggle it along with Owen and Billie. The shop was filled with floor to ceiling bookcases—gold, as far as I was concerned.

I was attempting to browse the rows of dusty books, when I suddenly remembered the recommendation from the Blessed Mother. "Do you have a copy of a book called, *A Song Of Prayer?*" I asked the girl at the counter. She began clicking away on her computer and came up empty. I thanked her and drifted towards a back corner of the shop. There were piles and stacks of all types of books jammed into overstock bookcases of eccentric sizes and styles.

I settled down into a sequestered corner of metaphysical books and began to peruse the shelves. Then I came across the most interesting title: *A Course in Miracles*. There were actually two versions of the book. One had only the text and the other contained all three sections, the text, the workbook and the manual for teachers. I knelt down on the dust covered wooden floor and examined the books to try and get an idea of what this *A Course in Miracles* was all about. I opened to the Introduction and read, from the preface.

The course does not aim at teaching the meaning of love, for
that is beyond what can be taught. It does aim, however,
at removing the blocks to the awareness of love's presence,
which is your natural inheritance. The opposite of love is
fear, but what is all encompassing can have no opposite.
This course can therefore be summed up very simply in this way:

Nothing real can be threatened.
Nothing unreal exists.
Herein lies the peace of God.

I closed the book, and promptly took both volumes to the cashier and purchased them. I did not know anything about *A Course in Miracles* and I had no idea why of all the books in that over stocked shop I left with not one but two volumes. I did feel that these books would have an important impact on my life. I'm not sure how I knew this, but there was no need to question, and that alone brought me peace. The Course was already having its way with me.

Looking back I see clearly why I was drawn to buying not one but two copies. In the years to follow I would not just study *A Course In Miracles,* I would be asked to teach the Course in many different settings and in many different classrooms. Having two volumes instead of one would make that teaching a lot easier. I shoved those two volumes into my over packed suitcase, gathered up the kids, and we headed back to LA.

I began to read and study the concepts of ACIM. It gave me a radical new way to be in the world and I was desperate to find other people who were studying this book. There were not many at the time so I just began sharing what I was learning with friends and family. I was impressed with how applicable and yet startling these concepts were. I was amazed at how equally these ideas of loving more and fearing less could be applied to everything. Mostly I loved that in order to share these spiritual principles, I didn't have to be anything different than what I was. There was no special handshake, no permission slips and no jump through any hoops.

"A teacher of God is anyone who chooses to be one." Like the Twelve-Step Program, it encouraged the idea that in order to fully embody these principles, I simply had to give them away.

The principles made sense with everything I had learned so far. I had been studying Science of Mind and Twelve-Step concepts, so it all could be immediately applied. I would read just a bit and experience a wave of peace. For whatever reason I was ready, and I began to immerse myself in it with a complete loyalty that I had never given to anything else.

It wasn't long before I received a request from a friend to start a study group, I didn't hesitate. My house was already a hub of activity, AA groups, writing groups, and now *A Course in Miracles*. It was at one of the first Course gatherings that a new friend came to join us. Before we even got started, she handed me a small thin book.

"If you really want to know about A Course In Miracles this is the most important book you will need." I looked down at the pamphlet in my hands and read the title, *The Song Of Prayer*. The book that the blessed Mother had suggested all those years ago on the moonlite hill in Yogoslavia.

Could it be that the book found me? Came right to my door? I have no doubt that clearing my consciousness through forgiveness and the purification of my body through sobriety helped to usher in greater synchronicities with greater grace. This was truly a miracle.

— TOOLS —

Come Clean

We all have places in our lives where we have graduated and yet we are still holding on. In order to grow we have to let go and be willing to burn the crops of yesterday. When your cups and cupboards are full, it's hard to receive or be in the flow.

It's time to contemplate what is really possible for you in this second breath of life. Like the old newspaper we have infinite possibilities. We each have a thousand more chances, a million more lives . . . but first we need to come clean, confess the harder truths, burn the old crop and let it set us free.

Creating tribes and joining with like-minded people can usher in radical changes that would take years longer if you were to go it alone. It's time to come clean and call in your midwives and wingmen.

Traveling companions make the trip. They are also helpful in seeing your blind spots, watching your back, and encouraging you in the rough patches.

These are the folks who you can trust to be there to witness when everything falls apart. These are the folks who understand that this mess is only a part of the delivery.

— DO THIS —

Come clean. You already know the ships that need to be burned. You know your blocks and your Achilles heal. As much as we want to go it alone, it might be time to get help from a group of like minded people who are in your corner. The early morning twelve-step group of poets and pirates, the mafia moms, these were my tribe and what I learned from them was priceless.

Whether it's over shopping, under earning, over eating, sex addiction, there are a million masks that the ego can hide behind and we all have a few. But with willingness there is help. There is a twelve-step program for everything from incest survivors to gamblers anonymous. These are sacred circles where you can show up, pay attention, and really tell your truth. Everyone in the world would benefit from a twelve-step program. These twelve sure and simple steps will walk you right out of hell.

Show up to your classrooms and invitations, pay attention to your teachers, whether they be called cancer or addiction or fame. It's all a classroom. Tell your truth, your hard and helpful truth. Love like you will not have another opportunity. You might not, and finally, don't forget to laugh. Don't be stingy with your happiness.

Who are your midwives, who are the people whom you can trust to hold your highest good? Who are your wingmen, the team that flies with you and helps you stay on course.

Write out a list of midwives and wingmen. If you don't have them, begin to write a list of people you would like to hang around with. Be specific, write out the characteristics and be aware of those types of people when they show up.

Even if you have only one good wingman or midwife, that is more than enough. Let them know that you have their back and get busy appreciating them. What you focus on increases.

Chapter 16

Celebrate Everything

This is the day when it is given you to realize the
lesson that contains all of salvation's power. It is this:
Pain is illusion; joy, reality. Pain is but sleep; joy is
awakening. Pain is deception; joy alone is truth.
—*A Course in Miracles*

To tell you the truth I was teaching A Course in Miracles,
which is a program of forgiveness, while I was still carrying a big grudge towards Reed. After Will and I got
married, Reed took me back to court to claim legal custody or
Owen and to change his name. It felt like a horrible nightmare
and I fought it with every cent and breath that I had and I lost.

It was during this time that my unforgiveness was at its
peek and as an alcoholic I had no budget for anger or resentment. I prayed. I prayed. And then I prayed some more.

After a few years of teaching the Course I received a calling to open my own church. It was a clear voice in my head, not too different from the one that told me to look into the side compartment of the car door. But this time the voice came with a picture.

Will and I had moved to the Chicago area and I was teaching *A Course in Miracles* out of a little office. It was the end of the year and I was facilitating a Visioning process. This was a process that was created by Rev. Beckwith from Agape Spiritual Community. The room was filled with women who were seeking a clarity of vision for their lives. I brought them into a meditation and began asking the questions.

"What is the highest vision for this year? What do we need to let go of to step into this vision? What do we need to embrace in order to step into this vision? Is there anything else for us to know?" I asked the last question and prepared to bring the ladies out of the meditation.

That was when I heard the voice. It simply said, "Going to the chapel," and along with the words, an image of a little white chapel popped into my mind. I saw it clear as day. So clear that I shared the vision with the room of women and I remember trying to figure out the meaning.

"Going to the chapel? What does that mean? Am I going to get married again?"

A week later the woman who rented the office across the hall approached me. She was a student of the Course and was a regular at my Wednesday night class. She was also a singing teacher.

"I think we should do a kids camp together."

"Okay."

"I'll teach the singing, and you will teach the acting, and if we get too big for our space, we can rent this old chapel." She handed me a pamphlet and on the cover was the very same little while chapel that I had seen in my head a few days earlier. I was speechless.

"I just saw this picture of the chapel in my head the other day," I said to her. "What does it mean?" She shrugged.

"It's a little church not far from here and it's for rent." I had no idea what it meant.

A couple weeks after that I was teaching *A Course in Miracles* in my office when it all became clear as a bell. So clear in fact that I blurted out to the room, "I am supposed to go to the Chapel and open a fucking church!"

The women in the room laughed not just because it seemed like an oxymoron, but because it felt as though I had stumbled upon a secret door and we all knew that we were going to walk through it together.

"A *fucking* church?"

A week later a small group of ladies joined me to check out the chapel. It was perfect and within the month I was running what would become known as SpeakEasy, a spiritual center based on the wisdom of *A Course In Miracles*. I did not actually become a priest because no matter how I tried, I just couldn't squeeze myself into a word that had no space for me and all my parts, especially my lady parts, of which I have a few, some of which have been purchased but they are mine nevertheless.

I struggled for a while to find the word that represented me and what I was. Just like my mother's name on the step, I eventually stumbled upon the exact word that perfectly encapsulated my calling.

When I found it, it was like finding Christmas morning in my pocket. There I was. Right there on the page, spelled out in letters that summed up the content of my being. In a word that was universally understood and accepted. I was so happy that I almost wanted to cry, but I didn't, because that is not what I do. What I do is celebrate and so I did. Which as it turns out was perfect because I am a *celebrant*.

Have you heard of this word? Do you know what it means? A celebrant is one who celebrates the deeper meaning of life. A celebrant is a spiritually trained, certified professional who is called upon to craft and create and perform high quality personalized ceremonies, services, and sermons for individuals, families, organizations and communities.

This is the thing I had longed to do as a little girl. I help to celebrate the passing of life's major events.

Some days I dress in ceremonial whites to perform a wedding or a baby blessing or officiate the celebration of someone's life at a funeral. Most days I am called to summon the sacred and sew a bit of wonder in the hem of life. To give a poetic nod to a memorial service, to bless a blushing young couple's vows. Basically, I get front row seats to life's most beautiful moments. I am asked to help usher these experiences into words and coax the sacred by reflecting the beliefs, wishes, and values of the individuals I serve. With a dash of the divine, a nod to cultural traditions and a wink of the whimsical, I weave the webs, that say, "This is who we are, this is what is happening and we want to be witnessed in our community." That's all people really want. They want to be seen. They want to be celebrated.

So I witness and celebrate things. I have celebrated married couples on their anniversaries and presided over recognition ceremonies for businesses. These moments are some of my best spent hours.

It is funny to confess that my training for these moments came from running that first business, Princess Parties. Everything I needed to know about being a celebrant I learned from celebrating little girls on their birthdays. It was a boot camp of sorts.

I remember preparing for those events, dressing in my special threads, Belle, Ariel, the little Mermaid or whatever princess the birthday girl wished to have in attendance. Thinking about that child and the fact that I was charged with making this day magical and meaningful. Playing music, telling stories, looking them in the eyes, letting them know that they were being witnessed at the crossing of this bridge that went from five to six or seven to eight. And that it was, in fact, very important and celebration worthy and that they were, in fact, very special and this day was one of great meaning and that was why I was there as Belle or Ariel or whatever princess was needed to bless the day.

I stood by and watched as they closed their eyes, tucked their chins, made their wishes and blew out their candles as I gave them a smile attempting to convey that I too believed their wishes were worthy and would reach the ears of God, or Santa or the stars or wherever the hell little girls send their wishes. What I thought was me trying to make ends meet was really God preparing me for my next chapter.

This, as it turns out was very good training for a celebrant. Not much is changed. I come with stories and songs and secret smiles and noble nods. I show up at rituals and rites of passage and ceremonies and blessings. I do my best to listen and deliver the message that is specific to the attendees to ensure that the day is artful and artisan, and woven with wisdom. It is my greatest joy to craft these personalized ceremonies that reflect the client's beliefs, philosophy of life, and personality. To allow myself to be an empty and open channel for the God of *their* understanding, whatever that may be and however that works for them. It's my honor and privilege to mark a unique moment or milestone in someone else's life.

The thing I have come to find in finding myself is that it is not just special segregated moments that are sacred. The mystical does not attempt to pour Herself into thimbles. She is in everything, every breath is sacred, every second divine, and all the rough hours as well. So I celebrate the bloody brawls that break out in funeral parlors and the secret baby bumps that lay beneath the bridal gown and all the other millions of ways that life vehemently refuses to wait for ritual.

I celebrate the divorced parents who have not spoken in decades but somehow against all odds arrive at the wedding of their child to witness her take part in the same institution that damn near broke them both and that breathtaking moment that sometimes happens when against their will their eyes accidently meet once more, and something slips out, not so much in forgiveness but simply a moment of truce, and that in itself is a miracle.

I celebrate the gay grandpas who arrive in dapper dress to pledge before the community and God that they will do all they can to help raise this child up. I celebrate that it is not lost on anyone the courage it takes when they themselves have suffered from the religious agendas that sought to bring them down.

It's the multifaceted beauty of our humanness that I celebrate and the majestic way that life holds so many sacred moments. This is the final suggestion that I have for you, dear reader. The invitation to step into your own enthusiastic celebrant. To practice the art of honoring. I encourage you to take the time to pause and notice the mystical in all things and have the generosity of heart to speak a reverent word when brilliance comes to call. This is a very small way to add big meaning to our little lives. This is the final tool.

Take the time to share a sacred word, sweep the mundane from your doorstep and reveal the beauty of the mystical. Celebrate the diverse tapestry of the human experience through your stories. Find the words that help you craft your own personalized prayers, court an intimate relationship with your Divine. Find the words that help you free your truth.

After all, words are so important, so find the ones that invite in the extraordinary, transform the common to the celestial, and bring a bit of heaven to earth.

⌒ FINAL TOOL ⌒

A spiritual vixen is a master celebrant. She loves with complete recklessness. She has no tolerance for anything less than unconditional. She has walked through fires and her scars are not hidden or praised but used to remember the escape route for others.

She answers the door to angels and demons with equal grace and curiosity. She holds an unflinching faith that everything will work out in the end for the highest good. She is fearless.

But of course YOU already knew all of this. The way you become a spiritual vixen is by simply deciding that your agenda is no different from you sisters. That your good is everyone's good.

Once you decide that this is your truth, you are at the place where you can claim and honor your spiritual maturity and authority. You have all the power you need to succeed. It's time for you to use these tools to carve yourself a kingdom, my sister, and rule it like a honest queen.

⌒ DO THIS ⌒

1: Connect with your Divine. The power of your presence is magical and vitally transformative, so before you show up to the ever changing current of the world's wants, needs, and agendas, the first invitation is to show up to yourself, your spiritual practice, and the directions of the Divine.

2: Ask for Signs and Symbols. Pick a sign, symbol or set of numbers that will remind you that you are on course with your optimal outcome. Ask your Divine to sprinkle your path with signs and symbols.

3: Take your time. If you can't do it in peace, don't do it.

4: Affirm your greatness. Your words will create the mundane or the miraculous, use them well.

5: You are Entitled. Look at the titles that you wear and imagine how you might play those roles in a more optimal and authentic way.

6: Invest in yourself. Listen to your heart and invest in yourself.

7: Showing up. Showing up is how you show the world what is important to you.

8: Tell your stories. Look at the events that have shaped you and begin to write, share and honor your stories.

9: Ask questions. Embrace your curiosity. Questions are the springboard to inventions.

10: Stretch and strategize. Cultivate joyful expectancy, write down your deepest desires. If money were no issue and you knew you could not fail, what would your perfect day look like?

11: Master the art of savoring. Express your happiness in an unapologetic way.

12: Embracing your fire. Remember that your anger is directional. Let your passion inform your platform and your massacres inspire your message.

13: Your Legacy. Write out your legacy and eulogy. Take an inventory of how you have already made an impact on the world. Celebrate yourself.

14: Be Kind to the universe. Be generous with your compassion. When given the opportunity, take the high road.

15: Come Clean. Do a burning bowl ceremony and consciously make space for a new crop.

16: Celebrate everything.

Acknowledgments

I wish to acknowledge Will Schaub, my husband, your love, constant support, encouragement, and humor has made this all worth it.

To my five sisters who have helped me live the best days ever.

To my children, Owen, Billie, Liam, and Rhine, for listening to my stories even when you pretended not to be listening. I only hope you heard the part where I said, "I love you." Because I do.

To Voice Box, my dear storytelling community and specifically Cathy Richardson who has brilliantly supplied the sound track to all our stories.

My students and teachers at SpeakEasy Spiritual Community, and Miracles Live 365 and all the sacred circles thank you for all that you have shared.

My publisher Brooke Warner, who gave me the courage not to fold. To Crystal Lee Patriarche for your faith and tenacity.

Special thanks to the generous editorial guidance of Lauren Wise, Megan Hannu, Elizabeth Keats, Claudette Sutherland, and Barbara Pierson Schaedel.

About the Author

Maureen Muldoon is a celebrant, writer, author, and spiritual vixen. She spent twenty years working in TV and film as an actress and writer. She lives in La Grange, Illinois and Madeline Island, WI with her husband and their four kids. She is the author of *Giant Love Song,* and the children's book *The Life of A Sandcastle.* Her poetry, personal essay, fiction, and creative nonfiction have appeared in *Story Lab, Lit Up, Booby Trap, Story, Actors Access, Voice Box, Risk!* and *Voyage Chicago.*

As an international teacher of *A Course In Miracles,* Maureen is part of the new generation of spiritual visionaries and thought leaders, she has trained top artist and executives in empowered leadership and communications, and has coached celebrities and media professionals, including Grammy and Emmy winners. As the founder and CEO of SpeakEasy Spiritual Community, an incubator of awesomeness, she shares cutting-edge spiritual principles and success strategies to achieve affluence, purposeful productivity, creativity, and happiness. From her global platform, Maureen has touched hundreds of thousands around the planet with her message on finding your voice, your path, your purpose and leaving your unapologetic mark of love. She blogs about creativity, spirituality, and storytelling at MaureenMuldoon.com where you can find out about her Celebrant Course as well as her other products. Be sure to subscribe to her Youtube channel for more insights and inspirations.

Author photo © Kate Webbink

⁓ WEBSITES ⁓

MaureenMuldoon.com
SpeakEasySpiritualCommunity.com
VoiceBoxStories.com
YOUTUBE https://www.youtube.com/user/maureenmuldoon1

SELECTED TITLES FROM SHE WRITES PRESS

She Writes Press is an independent publishing company founded to serve women writers everywhere. Visit us at www.shewritespress.com.

Loveyoubye: Holding Fast, Letting Go, And Then There's The Dog by Rossandra White. $16.95, 978-1-938314-50-6. A soul-searching memoir detailing the painful, but ultimately liberating, disintegration of a twenty-five-year marriage.

The Full Catastrophe: A Memoir by Karen Elizabeth Lee. $16.95, 978-1-63152-024-2. The story of a well educated, professional woman who, after marrying the wrong kind of man—twice—finally resurrects her life.

The Sportscaster's Daughter: A Memoir by Cindi Michael. $16.95, 978-1-63152-107-2. Despite being disowned by her father—sportscaster George Michael, said to be the man who inspired ESPN's SportsCenter—Cindi Michael manages financially and heals emotionally, ultimately finding confidence from within.

Green Nails and Other Acts of Rebellion: Life After Loss by Elaine Soloway. $16.95, 978-1-63152-919-1. An honest, often humorous account of the joys and pains of caregiving for a loved one with a debilitating illness.

Filling Her Shoes: Memoir of an Inherited Family by Betsy Graziani Fasbinder. $16.95, 978-1-63152-198-0. A "sweet-bitter" story of how, with tenderness as their guide, a family formed in the wake of loss and learned that joy and grief can be entwined cohabitants in our lives.

Falling Together: How to Find Balance, Joy, and Meaningful Change When Your Life Seems to be Falling Apart by Donna Cardillo. $16.95, 978-1-63152-077-8. A funny, big-hearted self-help memoir that tackles divorce, caregiving, burnout, major illness, fears, and low self-esteem—and explores the renewal that comes when we are able to meet these challenges with courage.